I WENT TO
COLLEGE
FOR
THIS?

I WENT TO
COLLEGE
FOR
THIS?

How to Turn Your
Job Into a Career You Love

AMY JOYCE

Washington Post
Career Columnist

McGraw-Hill

New York   Chicago   San Francisco   Lisbon   London
Madrid   Mexico City   Milan   New Delhi   San Juan
Seoul   Singapore   Sydney   Toronto

The *McGraw·Hill* Companies

ISBN 0-07-140010-9

McGraw-Hill books are available at special quantity discounts to use as premiums and sales promotions, or for use in corporate training programs. For more information, please write to the Director of Special Sales, Professional Publishing, McGraw-Hill, Two Penn Plaza, New York, NY 10121-2298. Or contact your local bookstore.

Library of Congress Cataloging-in-Publication Data

Joyce, Amy.
   I went to college for this? : how to turn your job into a
career you love / by Amy Joyce.
       p.   cm.
   Includes index.
   ISBN 0-07-140010-9 (acid-free)
   1. Career development.   2. Vocational guidance.   I. Title.
   HF5381 .J678 2003
   650.1—dc21

                          2002015417

This book is printed on recycled, acid-free paper containing a minimum of 50% recycled, de-inked fiber.

For my parents, who knew I went to college for something, and who always supported me no matter what. It just doesn't get any better than you.

And for Steven.

Contents

Foreword

I've always known that a game plan for life was necessary. Now that I'm 23, I see how important it is at each stage of life, especially that period right after college. This book by Amy Joyce is the best career book on the market for twenty-somethings, because it is written by someone who has actually lived and breathed the tales of work and career angst we all face as we head into the real world.

Amy shows how not only she, but how so many other twenty-somethings, have come out winners because they had a plan, believed that they could do it, and created a strategy for themselves. It's great to hear the stories of those who went before us. It gives me hope and makes me realize that the strategy I have talked about in my books for teens can really make or break us, both as we're living with our parents, and once we're completely out on our own.

Our parents—and yes, even my dad, the famous Dr. Phil— have all lived very different post-college lives than we do and we will. It's great to listen to their advice, but we have an entirely new world to deal with as we enter our twenties than they had. Amy's book reflects my philosophies that you can influence major parts of your life much more than you can imagine, not only in your teens, but especially in your twenties and beyond. This is your life, and your newfound, post-college freedom you have will allow you to have even more control over what happens to you. *I Went to College for This?* shows us that there is a reason for entry-level jobs, and that we have control over all those grunt duties many of us take on as we enter the world of work. We don't have to just sit back and take it; we can have control over our career life. Your twenties can be a wonderful time for exploration, as Amy says, and her book shows us just how frustrating, yet fun, it can be. She shows us, through other people's examples, how tough and yet rewarding a life strategy at this point in life can be.

I Went to College for This? is a great book to have on the shelf, both to help you come up with your own twenty-something life strategy, and to remind you that it has been done before by people just like you.

I know I will enjoy this book over and over again as I walk through my twenties. *I Went to College for This?* is a great collection of interesting tales and advice that we all could use.

JAY MCGRAW
Author of *Closing the Gap*

Acknowledgments

*L*ike many of the people in this book, I would not be here today without the generous help and guidance I have received during my years at work. Many thanks go out to the people who have crossed my path and left a mark. I've had too many Yodas to count.

Special thanks to Tracy Grant, for initiating Career Track and providing its young writers with patient editing and priceless instruction, and to Terry O'Hara, for swift and smart column edits, and for the early help on this book. And, of course, many thanks to Jill Dutt and the Washington Post for providing great opportunities and support. Fred Barbash, Shannon Henry, Linda Perlstein and many, many more encouraged me and helped me figure out how to get here. Thank you (to the third power).

Special thanks to Jan Miller and especially Michael Broussard, agent extraordinaire, and to Nancy Hancock and her cadre of smart editors and assistants at McGraw-Hill.

Thanks also to the friends and friends of friends (this could go on) who provided me with honest and insightful tales about those first years in the wild workplace.

Boundless appreciation goes to my family, immediate and extended, for the cheerleading. I truly am a lucky gal. And to Steven Ginsberg, for the edits, the constant support, the wise advice, and for missing that huge UVA game to read this manuscript for the thousandth time. Your support is above and beyond the imaginable. It's going to be a great life.

I WENT TO
COLLEGE
FOR
THIS?

1

This Is It?

*F*orget scheduling all your classes after 10 A.M. You have to use an alarm clock now—one that wakes you up earrrrly. Your tie looks too long. Your clogs definitely don't go with those tailored pants, young lady. And what's this about figuring out how to use public transportation during rush hour? Sigh. You don't even know if this job is right for you, or what the interviewer really meant by "administrative assistant." This whole life thing used to seem so much clearer.

When they asked you that age-old question in your younger years, "What do you want to be when you grow up?" you probably had an answer. Until you started to grow up. Then you actually began to think that maybe it wasn't so easy to just "be an astronaut." There's a lot more to getting a career than simply saying out loud what you want to do. It requires getting jobs to get that career. And, of course, figuring out what you want that career to be.

But that's okay. You're in a wonderful spot right now. Your twenties are a marvelous time to experiment, experience, and explore.

YOU DON'T HAVE TO KNOW IT ALL NOW

Before you freak yourself out, know that there is a super-rare, slight, not-really-going-to-happen chance that you're actually going to land a first job in that field you want. And there's an almost even rarer chance that you know what field you want to be a part of now—or 5 years, 10 years, or many years down the road.

I bet that doesn't make you feel any better if you're overwhelmed with this life-after-college thing, huh?

So what do you do? You try things. You apply to jobs that interest you. You talk to friends, family, and career counselors. You get out there. And with that in mind, remember that you'll get there. Most people spend their first 10 years in several different jobs, each one usually leading to the next bigger and better—and more YOU—job.

According to statistics and surveys, the average person will have 7 to 10 jobs before even leaving their twenties. Forget the stats; check out the real deal. Ask around. There aren't many people out there who actually stuck with a job they got right out of school, especially in our generation. With our parents' generation, sure, that was a little different. Many of our parents spent several decades with the same company, or even in the same job. And that's fine—for them. But our generation of twenty- and thirty-somethings has changed the way we work. Today, it's likely you'll switch jobs many times each decade, each one leading to something bigger, better, and more you. Today's newest workers view jobs as a way to figure out where to go, what to do, and how to do it, not just in a career, but also in life. We're rewriting the rules, and that's a good thing to remember. It's your career . . . so you get to decide what you want to do.

Colleen is 29 and has had five jobs since she graduated from the University of Virginia with a major in business in 1995. She realizes now that instead of planning each move, or consciously heading toward a new career path, she was running away from a job or situation that made her unhappy. It wasn't until recently that she took the time to sit down and figure out what it was about those jobs that she didn't—or did—like. She ran from those jobs because there was something about them that just wasn't right: She didn't get to do enough work, her boss was crazy, she took the job just so she could live in New York.

After some reflection, she was able to make a wise decision about her future. She knows that she wants to focus on housing and community planning for low-income families and communities, so she is now part of a graduate program to earn a degree in urban planning. And if it wasn't for her running away from a job at a bank, to a job as a teacher of inner-city students—where the seeds of thought about her future were planted—with a few stops along the way, she wouldn't be at this turning point now.

She's not alone. There is 27-year-old Lisa, politics major, turned legislative aide for a congress member, turned public relations manager for a New York marketing consultancy. And 28-year-old Alison, another politics major, turned technical writer, turned production manager, turned documentation manager at a dot-com, turned public relations coordinator at a telecom association. And she's also about to apply to graduate school for an MBA. Jonathan was a congressman's aide, worked for a think tank, got a job at the White House, then quit it all to compete in the Ironman Triathlon and try his hand at journalism. Today, he's a 29-year-old freelance writer. Lisa, 28, was an art history major, turned assistant at a consultancy, turned saleswoman at a start-up, then a software firm, and finally (for now) another software company. And 27-year-old Cara, an education major until senior year, who switched to speech communications before graduating. Then she spent her first summer as a teacher at a camp in San Francisco, returned to New York and got a job as a data entry specialist at a financial services firm. Then she went back to school for a master's in cultural communications but decided it was too expensive. Being that she had no specific career plan at the end, she moved to Washington, D.C., worked at Georgetown University's alumni relations, then temped for four months, then moved to San Francisco for a job at a dot-com, then moved to another dot-com that went belly up, then took an entry-level job at a telecommunications firm . . . and now she is interviewing because she wants to get into nonprofit work.

Whew. And just think about all the others out there who took some chances, spent their twenties exploring the myriad options available. You certainly don't need to know now where you might want to end up. But each time you are about to take a step, try a little self-analysis. Do I really want to be a part of this company? Do I really want to do data entry for a bank? Would I rather be a teacher? It's okay if you take some jobs that might not necessarily be your thing. Just make sure you learn from each step along the way.

So how did the people I mentioned, and the trillions of other graduates who went before you, figure out where to go first? They did what you can and should do: Take some time to think about things, and use as many resources as you can—your college career center, your internship colleagues, your professors and friends. Start reading the want ads, and take special note of what piques your interest. You probably already have a decent idea of where to go. As in, you know that you don't want to do anything math-related, so applying to an accounting firm probably isn't going to be your first love. Go with that instinct.

WHERE TO START?

Sometimes you don't know what you want to do until you experience it.

Hillarie Fogel's first weeks out of college were spent sitting on her mother's bed, checking out the want ads. With a degree in psychology, she answered a help-wanted ad to be an assistant at the Chemical Manufacturer's Association. No, she had no clue what that organization did; she hadn't taken a chemistry course in her life, and she had no idea what she was going to do in an assistant position. But that job led to her love for public relations.

And so with the help of a mentor (with really great people skills), she learned how to do things like make a room full of middle-aged Texan men laugh. She learned about deadlines. And she learned how to network. One year into her job, she moved to the organization's communications department. And then after meeting someone from the American Chemical Society at a local meet-and-greet event for people in the chemical industries, she was offered a position in the newly revamped communications department. Her first pitch to a reporter ended up as a front-page story in the *Boston Globe*. Then in her late twenties, she got a great job in public relations at Deloitte & Touche, a mammoth consulting firm.

And then, she got laid off. So you might think Hillarie feels like she is starting all over again. Well, she doesn't. She knows what she wants to do, at least to some extent, and she's allowing herself some time, again, to figure that out in finer detail. In the meantime, she's helping her boyfriend paint houses, so she can earn some extra bucks. Yep, the guys at the gym know her now ("Hey, you still haven't found a job?" one recently asked her), but she's getting somewhere. And better yet, she's been somewhere. She knows that she loves public relations and will stay in it in some way.

So how do you get from recent college grad to pretty durn happy with a job?

NOTHING'S TOO SMALL FOR THE RECENT GRAD

First off, know that it's not a bad thing to be in a base camp that leaves you yearning for the top of the mountain. There are a lot of entry-level jobs out there that can be fun and can lead to What You Want to Be When You Grow Up. These first few years out of school may leave you with a permanent callous from using the stapler so much, but remember that these first jobs are just the beginnings of a fulfilling life and career. These first jobs will help you decide what you like to do and, in many ways more importantly, what you don't like to do. And I know you've heard this already, so I won't dwell, but there are dues to be paid.

When my friends and I started out in our first jobs, some of the things we had to deal with were rather strange. One friend who worked as an aide on Capitol Hill for a senator had to wear business suits even if Congress wasn't in session, even if no one was in the office, even if she was packing boxes.

I had to ask permission go to the bathroom.

Another friend took a job in human resources but was asked to fill in for the company receptionist to answer the main phone lines during lunch hour, probably just because she was the youngest one in the office.

One young woman had to take her boss's SUV through the car wash every week. Never mind that her five-foot-tall frame felt overwhelmed in the vehicle, and was scared to death to drive her boss's über-expensive car, especially through a car wash. Of course, it's not all bad. Some of these first frustrating moments are a perfect time to let yourself figure it all out. And nothing motivates a woman to make a career decision like sitting in a car wash with Mr. Big's gas-guzzler.

Yes, you will likely be spending a lot of time with Xerox, your new best friend whom you will soon hate. You will gain the unenviable skill of unjamming the machine. You will figure out that to lengthen the life of a toner cartridge all you gotta do is shake it. These sure don't seem like things you learned in college and certainly are not what you hoped to do with a degree in politics. But here you are. There's a reason for it, and you will figure out that fine line of when you shouldn't say no and when it's time to start saying no. (We'll discuss that later.) But let yourself realize there is life beyond the Xerox machine, and you will get there, eventually. In the meantime, do the best you can without whining, or the time at The Machine will just be that much more difficult and torturous.

TAKE IT FROM SUE

A few years ago, Sue Schulz graduated from Loyola in Baltimore with a degree in English. Upon almost-graduation, she realized that journalism might be her thing. She liked to write, she liked to be published, and she spent several years on her college newspaper. She had a particular interest in magazines. Her dad's friend worked in journalism and sat down to tell her that she would likely have to start at a trade publication first, before she could move on to something a person could actually buy in a bookstore. She didn't like that prospect.

Luckily for Sue, her sister knew someone who worked for *Entertainment Weekly*. (And here is where I tell you to keep reading. We'll talk later about how to use your family and friends to network and find jobs.)

Sue talked to the person at *Entertainment Weekly* who was hiring, and she promptly landed a two-week fill-in position to cover for a clerical assistant who was on vacation. Fine by Sue. As temporary as it was, a paycheck is a paycheck, and she figured two weeks at *Entertainment Weekly* was a good start on her road to magazine journalism and would be a notch on her résumé. So she headed to what was supposed to be a short two-week stint.

Of course, the assistant she was replacing came back. But Sue apparently did such a bang-up job of phone answering and taking care of the seemingly little duties that were asked of her, no one wanted her to leave. So her supervisors (which really counted as everyone at the company) found odd jobs for her so she could stay on. Sue knew that if she fixed the fax machine promptly, if she helped her boss with a filing project, and if she did that grunt work that no one else wanted to do—without complaining or acting like it was beneath her—she would be recognized as a potential professional, or even a professional with potential.

Plus, doing good grunt work for everyone helped her to meet people, learn what they do at the company, and make pals with a few people who could help her move into something she would rather do.

"That was the way I made my contacts. They had all these other things that never get done," she says. So she offered herself up to anyone and everyone who needed, well, just about anything. She knew that if she was cool with the little things they asked her to do, she would be deemed useful. She also knew that the first few weeks out of college was the time to do the seemingly unimportant things as best she could. Because in the end, the way she handled herself and those jobs really did matter, even if she didn't realize it right away. (More on that epiphany next chapter.)

It ends up that Sue's main job, basically, was to maintain celebrity files. Every day, she looked through the gossip columns, photocopied items related to a celebrity, and put that clipping into a file. "It was kind of silly in a way, or so I thought at the time, but I realized after being there for a while that when the writers went to interview a celebrity, the first thing they always did was get the file." All of a sudden, those daily minutiae took on some sort of meaning and importance. Hey, everything has to get done, right? So why not make that go-to person be you? At least for a little while.

The files, such a seemingly silly job to do at the time, were the basis of what so many of the magazine's journalists depended on before heading out for an interview, which eventually turned into a story in the magazine. If the files weren't maintained, or were put together in a sloppy manner, Sue's coworkers wouldn't be able to do their jobs (jobs she someday wanted), and they would immediately know who screwed up. But by maintaining the files properly, Sue was assumed to be a competent young worker, no matter how minor her duties.

There is a time in just about everyone's career when they feel they are doing things at work that are way beneath their level—

beneath their education, experience, intelligence, and creativity. It's not a bad thing to feel that way; in fact, those feelings can push you to go after what you really want. But those beliefs can also hinder you if you bitch about grunt work you are asked to do, and you don't focus on why you're doing the things you do and how to turn these duties into a good opportunity.

I personally also thought there was a lot more out there for me than phone answering. And there was. I knew that, and that's why I stuck it out. My enjoyment of the place where I worked, the *Washington Post*, went way beyond any frustration I had at spending my day chained to the desk. Although the grunt parts of the job drove me to tears at times, it was the excitement of that atmosphere around me, the opportunity to talk to and work with some amazing people, and the knowledge that I probably wouldn't be answering phones forever that pushed me to go to work relatively happy everyday.

If you make the best coffee, if you get your boss's files organized a day ahead of schedule, or if you keep celebrity files up-to-date for journalists, you're doing things. And trust me, these seemingly little tasks do not go unnoticed. Even if you are not thanked regularly for the things you do (which you shouldn't be), your boss knows that you are a competent person. Granted, sometimes you have to make sure your boss notices, perhaps by mentioning that you finished the filing she asked for or by asking people who praise you to mention it upward. But your boss will know you are doing well, or at least will hear it from the others around you. Then, when the time comes for a promotion, a new job, or a good reference, you'll be ready to ask and receive. (See the sections on "Asking for More and Better" and "Salary Negotiation Time" in Chapter 3.)

These first jobs—whether you are in a true grunt job like Sue was or in an entry-level job that doesn't include faxing and filing—will lead to something. It's up to you to do a great job and figure out what that something will be along the way.

Sue realized about six months into her job that by working hard, she was movin' on up. That's because she went from clerical work to a real, live project. *Entertainment Weekly's* parent company sent her to *Time magazine* to do some temporary clerical work there as well. So Sue split her time between the two magazines. About six months after she landed the original job, she was asked by some people at *Time* to produce a fold-out poster of all 148 breeds of dogs that were part of the Westminster Kennel Club Dog Show.

Why was Sue handed the project? Maybe her boss didn't want to do it. Maybe her boss was too busy. Maybe her boss wanted to help Sue move in the direction she wanted to go. Either way, Sue was given a project that would appear in the magazine. It was, as many jobs for us twenty-somethings can be, random.

But it was all hers.

"I had to take a list of the people who were signed up to come to the show and pick one owner of each breed at random to come in for a photo shoot," she says. And she had to do it in a way that the selected owners were psyched to do it, but would not brag to their competitors who were not selected. It may sound like a trivial issue to some, but it was one of the trickier parts to her assignment. (There's big envy in the dog show world, apparently.)

Sue was excited on many levels. First, it showed that her boss assumed she could take on more than celebrity files and phone calls. Second, she knew she would learn a lot by trying to figure it out as she went. And third, that whole confidence boost thing is pretty pertinent in these situations. "My boss gave me this project and she was like, 'Figure it out,' and I did. That was interesting. I think I learned that a lot of what you learn is getting something and winging it."

To learn by actually doing is a great way to figure out how things are done. Baptism by fire, on-the-job training, learning by doing . . . call it what you will—many times, real-life experiences are much more pertinent to your growth than any training program or college course. Sometimes you don't realize all you've gained until you look back. But it is helpful to try to discern what you're learning in the process. The more you realize what you're gaining, the more you won't assume that you're stuck in a bad job.

Sue had quite a day when it was time for the shoot, which took place during the dog show. Dogs were barking and being groomed endlessly. People were running around, stressed out of their minds because they found a broken nail on their poodle. In the midst of the craziness, Sue had to find the dogs they had signed up for the shoot and make sure each dog got escorted to the right place for the shoot. In the midst of this, she learned a little biology lesson. Some of the dogs were in heat, so she had to find out what dogs couldn't go near other dogs and make sure to schedule them at a different times. This is the glamorous life of a magazine employee.

"It was definitely an experience, and I'm glad I did it," she says. Sue still has that poster and, in fact, hung it on her wall at many of her jobs that followed. It's a great reminder of where she came from, how her hard work on something that she could have blown off really was important, and it was the beginning of great things.

From Xerox Maker to . . .

Dan Sondhelm first graduated from American University with a degree in finance. After finding the job market for a finance major frustrating, he decided to go back to American University to get his MBA in marketing. He soon landed an internship with a small financial marketing firm outside of D.C. and spent his days on various projects—from Xeroxing to FedExing to sitting in on conference calls. Yep, it's true. He was brand new to the company and the field, and he knew it. So he took the time to do those things he knew he had to do as an entry-level person. Sure, they were a little below both his education and his experience level, but he acknowledged that these were jobs that the new, young employees had to take on. He also knew that he could make opportunities for himself to move beyond the Xerox machine between his grunt duties.

He didn't push himself to the forefront but rather just showed an interest in the work. He was a lucky employee, because his boss wanted her interns to learn the business in addition to the grunt work. And she hoped that they would return when their MBAs were complete. "She wanted us to grow as quickly as we could," Dan says, in part because she knew that bright, eager students could soon be bright, full-time employees. Dan was also lucky in that the company was very small when he started. Only five people worked there. So his voice was heard when he asked to sit in on conference calls, he asked questions about things he read and heard, and he talked to the president of the company—who was his direct boss—about the financial industry.

Had Dan not shown an unquenchable interest in the business and really taken a few chances along the way, he might still be at that copy machine now. He feels that it definitely took some hard work and reflection to get to the point he is today. "You've got to start from the bottom," he says. "Listen to the conversations around you. Don't just fax that letter. Figure out what it is you're faxing. Don't just do the research. You figure out what the research means before you hand it to the boss. It's okay not to know all the answers. Ask questions both internally and to the clients. They want you to learn, so just try and learn as much as you can."

It wasn't as easy as it sounds. Just two months after he was hired, his company sent him to a financial services conference in D.C., where he was instructed to meet people, ask how the company could help them, and in general make good contacts and give the company a good name. He was supposed to form ties with financial companies, such as mutual fund firms, so his organization could then include them in their public relations outreach. Not bad for a copy boy. Dan showed immense enthusiasm to try new things, so attending the conference was approached with the same zest and determination.

Dan didn't yet completely understand the industry; in fact, he was so new, his feet weren't even yet wet. When he showed up to this conference, it was a nightmare. People told him they were too busy to speak to someone with so little knowledge of the industry. They didn't want to waste their time on such an inexperienced young person. Dan, who was only about 23 at the time, didn't want to go back the second day. "My business card didn't even have a real title under my name. When people asked me what I do at my company, what was I supposed to say? 'I fax and file?'" After a night of bonding with one little group of people over a few too many drinks, he did return. It was much of the same, but a little better. Now, almost seven years later, he swears it has gotten easier. Well, thank goodness. Today, he spends much of his time creating conferences himself and speaking to large groups of conference-goers.

As much as it sucked, and as much as he still feels uncomfortable at networking events and conferences, he knew that he could only get better at it, and more comfortable, if he kept going. He lived by that whole dust-yourself-off-and-get-back-in-the-saddle kind of adage. And it just happened to work.

So, okay, he probably wouldn't still be at the Xerox machine today if he didn't do those things, but he also wouldn't be a 29-year-old partner in the firm.

2

First-Job Frustrations

*M*any times, first jobs sound a lot better than they seem when you actually start working. Don't fear: Almost everything can lead to the next big thing. So it may not be that great when you have to make the coffee in the morning before anyone gets to the office. But it's about more than just the coffee. It may feel like this is *not* why you spent four years slaving over papers and case studies. But take a deep breath before you run off to join the circus.

Heather Siegel also knows your pain. After Heather graduated from Northern Arizona University, she trekked to Washington, D.C., to take on her—ahem—dream job. She had landed a three-month internship at a major leader in her chosen field of public relations. After working hard for those intern months, Heather convinced the company to hire her full-time, which they did. And they gave her the nice title of Account Coordinator.

Apparently, in layperson's terms, that means envelope stuffer, box carrier, and travel arranger.

"It was a little bit more of a disappointment than excitement," Heather now admits. She was stuck with what she considered to be "very remedial tasks." Looking back on it, in fact, she laughs.

Early on, her boss asked her if she would be interested in attending a large public relations event in D.C. Nervous and excited, Heather's mind raced to what she could do to prepare herself, and what suit would look most professional. A short while later, however, her boss peeked over the cubicle wall and mentioned, "Oh, and make sure to wear shorts and a T-shirt. You'll be unpacking the press materials."

See? You're *so* not alone.

Don't despair. I know your talents are being wasted. But if the organization is what you've always hoped to be a part of, then use and think of this sometimes-demoralizing time as an opportunity—even if that opportunity isn't close in sight while you're bandaging your day's paper cuts.

Now why, exactly, are the box-carrier and gossip-clipping jobs important? There are so many reasons; it's hard to know where to begin. So perhaps I should tell you where these jobs ended: Sue, at 30, is now a senior editor at *CosmoGirl*. Heather, at 25, has a fulfilling job in public relations with the Multiple Sclerosis Society, and 29-year-old Dan is a partner at SunStar—the same firm where he began life as an intern.

But these twenty-somethings didn't just end up with these great careers. They worked to get there, and there were many stops along the way.

FIRST-JOB BLUES

First jobs—and sometimes many beyond that—can be frustrating. Even downright depressing. We've got that subject covered. Many of us look back in agony on our first days and months in the workplace and wonder why we just spent three weeks gathering information for a database that won't be used or frustrated that our degree has led us to, well, *this*.

It's normal to have first-job blues, but it's also important to work through those blues and to listen to them. If you're pretty upset about your job the majority of the time, you may need to look in other directions for work. But what's probably more likely is that you are left, from time to time, depressed and not thrilled like you thought you would be. More often than not, you probably just have to accept and understand that first jobs can be a little disheartening if you let them. But also remember that you won't start at the top.

Think about the times that you are less than thrilled with work, and ask yourself why you're blue. Is it fixable? Is there an end in sight? Are there just a few things that make you upset, which will likely end in a few months? Sometimes it takes a while to work through the drudge and find your niche, or a little silver lining, in first jobs.

Rachel Brown had the blues. The 22-year-old's first project at her new job with a large consultancy in Atlanta was to call a few hundred golfing students to ask them to fill out a survey of questions about golf shops. She was hung up on, she had to pull long hours so she could catch people at home, she *hated* telemarketers and surveys, and the fact that she was the perpetrator herself was really demoralizing. And she had just graduated from Harvard with a degree in history. Yes, Harvard. "It felt like something a high school dropout could do," she says. "I cried a lot." For a week, she wondered why the hell she came to this godforsaken place. Sound familiar?

But Rachel knew she had to get everything done, so she dealt with her frustrations in several ways. First, she wrote an email to the staffing coordinator but DID NOT SEND IT. It detailed all the things she hated about the job and why she hated these things. Rachel made sure not to put the woman's name in the address of the email, just in case she accidentally hit Send. Even though she started to write the email thinking it would go right to the coordinator's in-box, Rachel soon realized that she should save it and look at it the next day after she cooled off a bit. Good idea. Had she sent it, she would have looked like a complainer and a hothead. Not a good idea. So, by writing out her frustrations, she was able to analyze what she could change, what she could talk to her boss about changing, and what she might just have to accept.

Then, to get through the project from hell, she set definable goals for herself, crossing out each day on the calendar as it passed. Not the ideal situation, but it did get her through. As did talking to other newbies at the company. She heard that their first projects were pretty cool, so she knew she had that to look forward to, because the first projects everyone is assigned are sort of the luck of the draw. "I realized I just had to get through it," she says. "I just said this might suck but kept remembering why this was a job: I was learning something." And she knew that just because this one project wasn't good didn't mean they all would be not good. "I'm the low man on the totem pole. It'll get better," she realizes. And in fact, it already has.

This is Rachel's first job out of college. It's all right, but it's not what she wants to do with her life. Of course, she doesn't know what that is yet. But in the meantime, she's learning a few things that she knows she'll be able to take with her in her future. And she's learning a few other things . . . such as what she *doesn't* want to do with her life.

PAYING YOUR DUES

So, what if you're new or an intern and you want to do bigger and better things? Don't be afraid to ask. It's up to you to take an active role in your career. Don't wait around for someone to tell you you're doing a good job. Don't sit at the desk and hope someone will ask you to help him or her with this next awesome project. Go after it yourself.

But, remember, no one is going to want to give you bigger and better work to do if you don't do your first job well. Do that job as well as is humanly possible, and you might be able to have a hand at something you'd rather be doing.

Sue Schulz, who spent much of her early days doing stuff that she didn't necessarily think was what she should do with a college degree, figured out pretty early on just how important her work was. And now, when she hires interns herself, she can't stand people who ask in interviews when they can start writing. "Entry level is entry level. When you show me you can make a really good freaking Xerox copy and deliver it to who I need you to deliver it to, then we can think about writing. Someday. But if they can't follow a simple direction because they didn't listen, then I won't trust them with this bigger thing. They already think 'I don't need to be the reporter; I need to be the writer.' It's not bad to have an idea of where you want to go, but be willing to take each step." Sue likened the job movement to little kids who are learning to walk up the stairs.

Some will put a foot on one step, then put the other foot on the step above that and tumble down because they tried to take too many steps without gaining any balance. The kids who learn to walk up steps without falling put one little foot on a step, and then put their other foot on the same step, then continue on.

One day, when Sue was at *Entertainment Weekly*, she got frustrated at her life. She was sitting with a newspaper, clipping out gossip columns on big name celebrities . . . something a first-grader could do. "At first, I sucked it up, but I was like, 'I went to college for this?'" (Hey, that would make a great book!) Then she sort of had an epiphany, thanks to Snoop Doggie Dogg. "I had clipped, like, eight things on Snoop. Then three weeks later, we had a story on Snoop, and I knew that file I did had somehow prepared the reporter for the interview, and the story was in the magazine. You stop thinking about it like 'I went to college for this' and then think 'this is an essential part of what this organization does.'"

Making a copy for an executive is not B.S. work, she says. She couldn't be more right. That executive probably needs that paper to take to a meeting. If she didn't have that paper, she might not have her information on hand that she needed to win a new client or get rid of a money-losing venture. And of course, it is über-important for you to be enthusiastic about it. You don't need to be a happy, happy, joy, joy cheerleader every time you are asked to do something. But if you get it done without whining, and you get it done correctly and quickly, you will be recognized as competent.

When Sue moved on to *Redbook magazine* as an assistant to two editors, that epiphany helped her get through her days, and happily. "I felt that when my boss did her job well, it's because I did well. Putting that investment into it, thinking that way, it was like it's not about me at that point. By it not being about me and about my self-worth, it was more of an investment in my future success. People were like 'she's good; she knows what she's doing and she can do it.' It wasn't all about me shining, so I shined."

. . . AND GRUNT WORK CAN BE WAY COOL

Sid McCain would have to agree with our friend Sue.

Sometimes being the low man on the totem pole can be a great thing. You're on the front line; you're the man with a plan, the jeans-wearin'-hear-everything-meet-everyone person. It can be great, and the guys in the big offices don't get a chance to be a part of it. So as much as you can, enjoy it. And remember why you should be enjoying it.

All Sid McCain knew when she graduated from Long Island University in South Hampton, New York, was that she wanted to do something with music and live in New York City. She had majored in photojournalism, but, well, you know. She had had a pretty cool internship with MTV, and maybe she was bitten by the pop-rock bug.

Around graduation time, she heard from a friend in the music industry about a job for a receptionist at a record company in the city, and she applied. "I think the expectation when you come out of college is 'I'm going to be the head of the department,'" she says. But she knew better. She knew she would ease her way in, check out the scene, and see how she did and what she thought of the music industry. She had no idea where to start and didn't have a clue as to how many different aspects there were to the music industry. Starting out on the front lines would probably be a good start. Never in a million years did she expect her first job as a receptionist to be so exciting—almost to the point of giddiness.

Sid's first week on the job left her sitting at the front desk, answering calls, helping people who had appointments—just the general taking care of business that goes with being a receptionist. But during the first week, rock megastars AC/DC were in town to do interviews. "I thought this was awesome. They sat in the conference room, and Angus Young just chatted with me." Talk about wide-eyed and psyched to be a receptionist. She and Angus chatted and became buddies that week. He would hang out in the reception area to chill out, and Sid was the perfect person to chat with. She's not very shy—in fact, she is quite outgoing—and that really helps her in the industry, she knows. During that first week, she and Angus Young walked down the street to get a couple slices of pizza. He tried to pay with a $100 bill, but the pizza shop didn't have the change. That stands out as a very "wow" moment of Sid's first job.

And this was called a grunt job? Ha. She'll take it.

ENJOY THE RIDE, YOU'LL GET THERE

As with any job, Sid had to take some steps along the way to get where she is now, but they were great steps almost the entire time. For one thing, she learned what she did—and didn't—want to do. And she learned a ton about her industry. She gained knowledge, found mentors, and met myriad rock stars . . . so many, she can't even remember them all. And she's only in her early 30s.

In general, she has nothing but good words about any receptionist job. In her experience, it is a perfect way to meet everyone at the company, high up or not so high up. As a receptionist, you can't hide. Also, your coworkers and bosses know that you likely have other dreams and don't plan to stay in the receptionist's desk forever, so it takes a little load off the office-hierarchy protocol. You can feel free to chat about your dreams to fellow employees who have time to stop by the desk. You can ask them about their experiences, learn a bit about the industry, and decide if you really want to stick with it, or if you might want to go in another direction.

"You definitely have to pay your dues," Sid says. But dues paying can be fun. Sid knew that, and also knew just how much she would gain from grunt work. In fact, she never once dropped her famous politician dad's name— John McCain— to land her in a better gig. Sid knew her dues-paying was going to pay off for her in the long run. In the meantime, not only did that time teach Sid a lot, it also meant free tickets to shows, interesting people, and conversations with everyone at the company, and she easily could learn what was going on around her. "It was awesome. I ate it up."

After the receptionist job, Sid was asked by another organization if she would like to try her hand at radio promotion, as an assistant. With the belief that it was a good new step, Sid took a sure-why-not attitude. As luck would have it, four months into the job, the company merged with another, and Sid got laid off. But she is serious about the "as luck would have it" part. It was a blessing in disguise. She pretty quickly realized that radio promotion wasn't her thing. Also, the former head of publicity from the old job asked Sid if she might want to come with her to Susan Blond, Inc., a mega-well-known publicity agency. Good idea. Had she let herself get stuck in radio promotion (which she swears never would have happened), she really would have missed out on a great opportunity.

Not long after she started at Susan Blond, Sid's boss left the company, which meant Sid got some excellent experience and was promoted pretty quickly. It helped that she had enough confidence in herself, and was outgoing enough, to just do it. "Everyday it was like, 'Oh my God. I get to work with Iggy Pop.'" She worked with Toni Braxton and got Morrissey on the cover of *Details* magazine. "I was really young and it was really, really cool."

In the midst of this incredible, busy, fun experience, Sid was offered a job to do publicity at another company with the woman who took her to Susan Blond. She turned it down and decided to keep doing what she was doing, for a while at least.

How did it happen that people were chasing her down to come work with them or for them, and she was only a few years out of school? Once you start to have successful press campaigns, people notice. But more than that: Once you do good work for someone wherever you are, people notice. Or they hear about you and your work, or guess that because you are so together and have succeeded in these other ways, you must be good. Even if those successes are as a receptionist or assistant to the publicist, it shows.

Sid has had a run of great jobs. After Susan Blond, she worked for several companies, getting better offers each time she took a leap. She now is head of publicity at New York-based record label V2 and loving it.

Now that she's sort of on the other side of the career line, she has some advice for those folks coming into the working world now. First of all, get over yourself. If you are asked to do a mass mailing, don't grumble and moan. Do it and do it well. Your work, attitude, and demeanor all will follow you. Sid said that if some of the interns who have worked for her had asked her to write a recommendation letter, she would say "no way," because they groaned when they were asked to do filings and faxings. "That's just part of the job," she says. And she really feels no pity for interns who have to do these seemingly piddling things. She did them; so can those who work for her. As a matter of fact, you can trust that most people higher up on the corporate ladder have done just about anything that you might be asked to do. Not only that, but it's pretty apparent that if you are not willing to put in some time now, that might mean you're not so into this career path.

When Sid first interned at MTV, she had to do the sandwich-getting, be a messenger to pick up things for story lines, and even had to run errands at 4 A.M. to make sure everything was set before the shows started. Sure, it could be a bit degrading, she said. But it was fun too. And if you are still having fun when you're running around with jobs that make you feel a little less fabulous, then it's likely you've found some nugget of career guidance to hang onto.

How did Sid decide she wanted to go into publicity? She still can't say for sure, except that it found her. "I didn't know what publicity was, but I took that first opportunity, and it turned out to be really great." Here's someone who truly loves her career. "It didn't happen overnight, but it happened fast enough."

3

Meeting People

*I*t's so easy to walk into your first job or jobs and feel like a stranger in a strange land. Well, you are. But you don't have to stay that way, and you shouldn't.

One of the advantages of that first job is meeting lots of people—primarily people with the same interests as you, or people who have an interest *in* you. (Your brains, I mean. We'll talk about office romance later.) These people you meet and impress in your early days might at some point help you to get that job of your dreams later on.

You have to remind yourself to kick your shyness curbside and introduce yourself. Just a little handshake will do. Ask the person who hired you, or your direct supervisor, to introduce you around a bit. That's the best way to make contacts, and then you'll know what to do and say when you bump into these people again.

Don't do what our friend Sue Schulz did (or did not do, rather) at her first gig at *Entertainment Weekly*. "That is one of my biggest regrets: I hardly talked to anyone at all when I was there. I was scared and intimidated and just thought people would talk to me first. For a long time, I was hung up on the thought that if someone was older, I respected them automatically. And even if someone started on Monday, and I started Tuesday, I just felt they had more experience. I just thought, 'I'm not going to talk to them first because it's presumptuous of me.' In the area I worked for four months, I hardly spoke to these people," she says.

"Of course now I realize that was the dumbest thing. If I could do that again, I'd remember that it's so important to not feel shy about introducing yourself. It's not like you have to be overly bold and obnoxious, ready to take over the place. Just introduce yourself and ask if there is anything you can do for them. That breaks the ice."

Sue believes that if she had introduced herself around a bit, there is just no telling what other opportunities or what other acquaintances she might have now. Not that she regrets where she is now at all. But had she talked to more people at her first job, "maybe it would have helped me get somewhere sooner," she said.

Starting out in an entry-level position lets you discover your talents and figure out the business—and much of that can be learned by those who went before you and those who work with you. Take the time while you're in this position to talk to those around you. They can be your greatest resource and can turn into your greatest asset. Don't be afraid to ask questions, to let them know what you might want to do with your life, to ask for advice and guidance. It can be tough if you're shy, and especially if you work in a large office where hiding is not all that difficult. But if you don't make contacts or don't talk to the people who may turn out to be a huge help to you, you're making your life much more difficult.

Albert Cevallos, 30, graduated from college with a major in peace studies. He hadn't taken on any internships before graduation, so he really didn't have any contacts in the work world. But he saw an advertisement at school for a job opening at the U.S. Institute of Peace. He went for the job interview—it was totally an administrative position. But he was absolutely fine with that because he was so excited at the prospect of being inside such an organization and around the people he knew were helping to change the world. He had to wait for several months before the organization knew if it would receive funding for the job. So after school, he waited tables while he waited for the call.

The call came, and he got the job. Albert's new boss said to him that the job would be entirely administrative, and it may feel like it's below his education and skill level. "But watch me, watch around you, and you'll learn a lot," his boss said to him at the time. "I'll never forget that," Albert says.

He did watch and even enjoyed his time stapling, filing, faxing, and answering phones. The best part about being there was meeting the interesting people who worked in Albert's dream career. "It opened so many doors. All of a sudden, I was working alongside ambassadors, war correspondents" and many others. Yes, he met them by faxing and filing for them, but he met them. Just one year later, he was hired as a research assistant for a war correspondent. Today, he is an independent contractor, and most recently, he went to Bosnia to do work for the State Department.

Just as Albert's story shows us, working in an entry-level job—whether that is a fax/stapling kind of job or a beginner computer programming job—can help you to establish yourself and your reputation. So as I've mentioned several times by now, have some patience. If you stick it out, you may later realize that you are further along than you thought, or people might notice that you paid your dues and paid them well. Especially if you asked these people questions or told them a little bit about yourself since you walked through that door.

Those who Albert worked with found he had a special interest in eastern European affairs. It just so happened that he was in their office just as the war in Bosnia began. That interest, which he clearly expressed to his coworkers, certainly helped him move up and out of that administrative position eventually. Of course, he likes to reiterate that he didn't hate the administrative work. It was a great way to talk to some of the most interesting people he ever thought he could meet.

Don't forget that entry-level or not, you are an employee, and these folks are your coworkers. Even if you're a temp worker or if you are truly the coffee-getter, that means you are a part of the greater organization. Many of these people you pass in the hallway can shed a lot of light on your murky future, but it's up to you to follow up on conversations or start them in the first place.

Once you start to make these contacts, don't be afraid to ask these people if you can help out on various projects and little jobs that interest you. You gain some experience; they gain an appreciation for you.

One twenty-something I talked to moved to the Washington, D.C., area with a degree in design. With rent and car payments looming, she knew that waiting for a design job much longer than the couple of months she had been searching just didn't make sense. So she went to a placement agency and got a job as a secretary. Fortunately, it was at a company that trained its administrative assistants in technology and Web design.

Pretty soon, she went from making coffee to division designer. But how? While she was there, she did good work at the job she was hired to do. But she also let her coworkers and supervisors know what she wanted to do with her life, and she let them know about her degree . . . not to the point of obnoxiousness, but enough so that they eventually felt that she should be doing more than secretarial work. She asked for them to think of her if they needed some extra design help. Soon her bosses let her have a hand at some Web designing. Piece by piece, she gained more trust, they liked her work, and she was promoted.

DON'T HIDE. STAND OUT—OR AT LEAST UP

There are a few ways to ensure that you don't fade into the background, that you can meet new people, and that you can share your new ideas while you're at an organization. It's important to show yourself and speak up, no matter how shy you are or how new you are to a job.

There are many ways to get yourself noticed at work. You could dye your hair 1980s purple, you could come to work every day in a different sling or cast, or you could put a Nobel Prize plaque at your cubicle.

You will probably find yourself in your first jobs looking up from your cubicle into a vast land of identical cubicles and wondering how the hell you can get yourself to stand out, how you can make yourself more than just a cog, how you can do something that you really want to do—and get paid for it.

You don't need blinking neon lights at your desk to turn your job into a great experience. But you do need to make yourself and your desires known. It helps to strike up conversation.

So what if you're the phone-answerer/newspaper-gatherer? Take the time while you're in a work environment to make yourself available. Learn from others, talk to decision makers, have coffee with that woman whose job you think is way cool. You'll be surprised by how many people are willing to give you advice and guidance or maybe even an email address for their best friend who heads up an organization you've admired your entire life.

You can start to get out there by getting to know people within your department with whom you have direct contact. So you're the coffee-maker? Take that morning wake-up time to tell the manager that you liked his most recent advertising campaign, and here's why. Start a conversation with your boss when he asks you to make 200 copies of the most recent study regarding public-speaking fears. Tell him why you're interested in this study and how that applies to the class you're taking every Tuesday night on public speaking. He would not have known that you'd be interested in making a presentation at the next board meeting unless you spoke up.

Without blowing your own horn too brazenly, make sure your voice is heard. Raise questions, voice concerns, express your own ideas. Even though you might feel like a little speck on the radar of your large organization, sing the song of yourself.

If you're a little too timid to voice your idea outright to the boss around the corner, how about an email? You have so much in your control (believe it or not); you can share your ideas—good ones—as much as you like. Things like email encourage folks like us to get our ideas out there. It even helps us to formulate the idea a little more clearly than if we were just speaking. Try to just write an email to yourself first. Once your idea seems clear (and smart), then send it to the manager or coworker you think should see it. Even if you just keep it to yourself, it can help you gain confidence to speak to someone about the idea later. Email is a great way, however, to get a point across without freaking yourself out too much.

A lot of people have great ideas but don't speak up when they have the opportunity. Then, lo and behold, the guy next to you expresses the idea and not only gets credit for it but also gets to work on the project. You sit there.

A new worker who views himself as too inexperienced to share his knowledge will be stunted in his growth. Not speaking up is only going to limit you—and, really, limit the organization as well. If you are one of the new workers who hide in the cubicle hoping no one finds you, but you keep doing a great job with the things that are assigned you, you're right: No one will find you. It's a big world out there, and as with anything, if you don't speak up, no one will know what you're capable of and what you're interested in doing.

Remember that you were hired for a reason. You're a part of the organization just like anyone else. Share your good ideas. Some may be taken lightly or blown off altogether, but others might be taken very seriously. And herein fits the age-old rhetorical question: What have you got to lose?

Not only will speaking up help you look better and gain you access to things and people you might otherwise not have, but it will also teach you and help you find the people who can help you grow. And it's your job to speak up. You're part of this world now, and your employers count on you- and your-brains to speak up. It's not the responsibility of managers to coax good ideas out of everyone. They don't have the time or the inclination for that; it's your responsibility. Now get out there, slugger!

DON'T EAT AT YOUR DESK EVERY DAY

Your first real desk (or cube, or space on a big table) at a company . . . it's a big deal. But don't let yourself get too used to it or too comfy with your ergonomic chair and corkboard wall. Even if you can surf the Internet during downtime, email friends, and play Minesweeper, sitting at your desk all day isn't going to help you meet people or find your Yodas (read on to understand what I'm talking about there).

What will help you is getting up to go to lunch. Getting coffee downstairs at the coffee shop or cafeteria. Asking your podmate if he wants to grab a bagel with you. It's good to get out, and if someone offers you a chance to do so, and you don't have to do any work immediately, take him up on it. Why? First of all, you never know when you might run into the boss. Yes, scaredy-cat, it's a lot easier to camp out at your desk. But when you see the boss and just introduce yourself, or say hi if she already knows you, you're putting yourself on her radar screen. And then she might notice your work more than if she didn't know you at all. Or she might check out what your direct supervisor has to say about you. Then, she may think of you when there is an opening at the one level above you. Get it?

That's what happened to our friend Sue. Even though she knows she did not talk to too many people at her first gig at *Entertainment Weekly*, she did get comfortable enough to chat with her direct supervisor, who came to know how well she worked. So when her supervisor's friend moved from *Enter-*

tainment Weekly to *Redbook magazine* and asked if there might be someone who would make a good personal assistant, Sue's supervisor suggested Sue as a good candidate. (And she did later interview and get the job.)

Amelia Zimmer, 23, has learned pretty early on that it helps so much to be outgoing and to force yourself to be outgoing even if you are a truly shy person. If you find yourself eating at your desk every day, force yourself to get out at least once or twice a week with someone at the office. It will help you find mentors, and it will let people know more about you—that there is more to you than your stellar faxing abilities. "If there are people going to get drinks after work or someone asks you to go out with coworkers, just do it. Don't pass up the opportunity to mingle with people," said Amelia. She makes sure that she joins in on the weekly company parties held in the office kitchen. It gets her in a good position to talk to people who have already helped her out in major ways. She has gotten contacts for people to talk to about new jobs, she heard about an opening within her organization, and hey, she has fun just chatting with people. "At office parties, don't go get your food and go back to your cubicle," she says. Yes, it's a comfortable thing to do, and I admit that I have been guilty of it, but when you do that, you miss out on interesting conversations, parts of which you might be able to contribute to and that might help you out in the long run.

Now that is just the casual hello side of the story. What about when the boss asks the team to speak up about possible ways to save money? Or wants ideas for a new ad design? Sometimes first-timers, or folks who are the newest members of the team, will hesitate to speak up. You might be afraid it's a bad idea or that someone else came up with that idea and you just weren't around to hear it. Or even worse, you might think you'll be seen as a suck-up. All unlikely. When you have an idea, share it. Even if you think you're too new or too young to share something to the whole team, and especially to the big boss, you need to take a chance. Of course, don't just blurt out the first thing that comes to mind. Think about it a bit, or even wait and come up with a better proposal the next time you meet for brainstorming results.

At the very least, and trust me on this, you will earn credit for trying. And big deal if your idea gets shot down. As a friend of mine likes to remind me, Joe DiMaggio failed more than 60 percent of the time, and he's in the Hall of Fame.

FOCUS ON WHAT YOU DO BEST

Even though you may be just looking for a job now or have only been in a job for a short while, you should try to focus on your main niche and what you specifically can bring to an organization that others may not be able to.

That is what 29-year-old Lilly did. As a teenager from Mexico City, she came to Miami to live with an aunt so she could attend high school in the States. From there, she went on to earn a degree in engineering. Through her years at college, she did several different internships with GTE and other wireless and telecom companies, and she discovered she really liked the burgeoning telecommunications industry.

After she graduated, she was offered a job with a telecom company that wanted someone with a technology background who they could also train to do sales. Not only that, they hoped to find someone familiar with Mexico and could do sales from an office there. Lilly excitedly agreed. So in her first year out of college, she was able to sell herself as someone who could speak fluent English and Spanish and knew the technology side of a pretty competitive field. She knew that using her language skills could be her niche in such a tight market.

"It was a tremendous jump for me . . . it would have taken 5 to 10 years to get there usually," she says of her job. But because she touted herself as having a special niche to help the company, she flew through the normal ranks that she otherwise would have had to plod through. Lilly was sent to Brazil for a while, and to Mexico for two years, and she was thrilled.

The fact that Lilly knew that her background and language skills could take her beyond just an average first job was a major bonus. While she was in school, she knew about this company and had wanted to work for them as soon as she could. She found out a friend interviewed at the company, but he only spoke English. He told Lilly that she should apply, and she jumped at the chance.

She did not shy away from telling recruiters about her language skills. That, coupled with great internships in a competitive industry, really helped her get some big jobs from the start, in an industry that she loves.

It is always that niche you discover, that special something you can do better than anyone (or at least get to before anyone else does), that will help you stand out and move on into some awesome jobs. I discovered pretty early on that as much as my young age in a place like the *Washington Post* could be looked down on, it also could be a major benefit. I began to write about young people's career issues (go figure). It was focusing on this that really helped me retain some credibility at the paper and allowed me to keep on keeping on, as they say.

It's easy to forget when you're starting out in this crazy world that you have some talents, or particular interests, that even more experienced people don't have. Don't forget to mention that your Walt Whitman honors thesis was published in a journal. Don't forget the awards you received in college, or that you are trilingual. Don't be afraid to speak up about a particular industry you think you should sell your company's product to. That can be your special gig, so that the company will find you indispensable. Even if you don't think these skills or interests are important, it's good to let people know you have them. Even if you get hired as an administrative assistant, let your boss know you speak Spanish. You may get some extra projects or be able to help on things you wouldn't normally be considered for, because you have a valuable skill.

STEPPING UP TO THE PLATE—WITHOUT STEPPING ON TOES

There is a need at some point to assert yourself and not just react to what's going on around you. Many times when we're new to anything, we defer to those who are more experienced or have been around longer. But there comes a time when we can be that person, to some extent at least.

Asserting yourself at work is a necessary thing, because this is your life and you can't just be reactionary, right? Of course, there will be some workplaces, some organizations, and some bosses that automatically allow people to assert themselves and do what they believe to be necessary when they think they should. And then there are the other workplaces where bosses are going to be . . . um, shall we say, reluctant . . . to accept your pleas, your desires, your ideas. Some bosses will subtly (or otherwise) not be open to your needs and wants. It's really hard to assert yourself and not make some folks mad.

DRAWING THE LINE

There comes a time when you do have to say no to some of these lowly tasks you're asked to take on. The first day is not the time. But as you continue down the workplace road a bit, you do have to pick your duties and learn when to say no. Nicely.

Sure, you want to make a good impression, be a part of the team, be the go-to guy. And it's easy to assume that if you do that, you'll be the superstar and get all the great projects. Well, there is a difference between being managed and being manipulated. If you always say yes when your boss asks you to pick up his dry cleaning, you're certainly not going to be viewed as the superstar. You're the hired help. Just because you know you have to do the cliché pay-your-dues thing, that doesn't mean you are bound to a life of servitude.

You have to learn when to say yes, when to say no, and when to bail to keep from sinking in a pile of projects and meaningless duties that are really not yours to take on. If you don't learn how to say no, you might miss opportunities that are a little more career enhancing than picking up your boss's dog from doggie day care.

If you say yes to everything that is asked of you, you're never going to have your own time, or you're only going to do all the tasks partly well. Like I said earlier, say yes, do what's asked of you, take on the grunt work with a smile. But there comes a time when saying no (in a nice way) will help you to gain respect in the eyes of your employer. You must, however, have a reason. Make sure when you decline a request to organize your boss's family photos into a collage for his wall, it's because you have something more meaningful to do for him—something that will actually make him think "Oh yeah, we all would be better served if she did some research on that rather than cut out pictures of Max." If you ask for more meaningful work or if you request a step up in your duties, your employer will view you as someone who wants more and who wants to provide more for the organization. It shows that you are interested in the organization and interested in learning and giving more. However, as with most things, there is a fine line between acting cocky and saying no in a professional manner. Keep in mind that your boss wants you to do well—not just for you but also for the company. So if you are getting too bogged down in grunt work, say that. But with a smile.

There is a way to make it clear your time will be better spent *not* doing all the grunt work all of the time. If your big issue is that your boss keeps asking you to run his pile of documents down to the office on the other side of the city, you can eloquently say, "You know, I'd like to do this for you, but I was asked to finish X. Is there some way we can get a courier to do it? Or can you suggest how should I prioritize?" Simply ask your boss to choose between your duties. If she wants you to finish writing the press release, which is expected to go out later that hour, she will likely see your point that you should not run across town; she will see (hopefully) that she and the company are better served by using your skills to write a press release than by having you run across town to deliver a package. If she is human, she will like that you're thinking things through rather than just saying yes to everything.

Sharing your aspirations will help you to cut down on the grunt work. It sometimes helps to express your interests without being asked. You can do this in your interview, or you can ease into it. Over time, you will begin to exude confidence. And with that confidence (not cockiness), managers will trust you for bigger projects and will overlook you when they need someone to make a doughnut run.

You really do need to share your aspirations with those around you. Don't talk them to death, but let people know that you are more than an entry-level person. You want more, and the more they know about what you want, the better chance you have to start moving where you want to go. People hear you when you mention that you want to be a reporter when you grow up to be a big person. They may not say anything then, but it's in the back of people's minds. And when someone needs something written, something that is beyond your job description, you might be asked to do it. Yes, because you're a good worker, but also because you show and tell them that you want to do it even before they actually need you. If you didn't share these goals, some decision makers might just glance over your desk when they scan the room for someone who might be interested in the next big project.

If you don't think you should be doing some of the piddling tasks you're assigned, tell someone. But don't whine and kvetch about the annoying aspects of the job. Use persuasive words like "I think I would be best used doing X. Is it possible that I could do that rather than this?"

Remember, though, don't take an attitude and just give an automatic no when someone asks you to come along to pick up a birthday cake for a coworker. Extra tasks often have some sort of perk, like making new contacts and gaining a good reputation with higher-ups. More often than not, if you say yes more often than no, managers won't hesitate to ask you to join in when something good comes along. They might even help you in the future, knowing you pulled through for them in the past.

ASKING FOR MORE AND BETTER

So we have learned something. First, make sure that most people know you can do a bang-up job in these seemingly low-rung positions. Then, feel free to ask if you can help on something that is a little bit above your job title.

Even if your position title doesn't change, you can attract better work. Set yourself up to be recognized as someone with great potential, like Sue Schulz, Albert Cevallos, Sid McCain, and the others did.

It may be hard to start doing these semi-aggressive things, especially if you're not a naturally aggressive person. That's when it helps to introduce yourself to people in the organization and ask questions. Find someone at your office who went to your college, look for someone who has the same interests or something similar to your background. Then cling, but not too tightly. Soon enough, you'll look back and realize that you were doing it . . . almost without even trying.

People at your organization will want to help. Talk to them. Let them know where you want to go, and ask that if they ever hear of something that you might be able to work on, they let you know.

Of course, you need to do the job you were assigned first. But working on extra projects during downtime is a good thing for all involved. Not only will it help you focus now, it will help you gain experience to win that next job or figure out what you want your next job to be.

You're in the job now, all safe and cozy. But there are a few things you need to know so you can navigate the office or organization to the best of your ability.

SALARY NEGOTIATION TIME

Everyone, minus a few masochistic souls, hates to ask for a raise. But it's unfortunately very necessary.

When we're new to the workplace, we sometimes are so excited to be offered a job that we just pant like puppies and bound off to call Mom about our great job offer—with the salary that means we have to live in an unheated efficiency apartment without a phone. Think before you accept the job. Know what you need to earn to live, and then figure out what you think you deserve, based on similar jobs and people of your position.

General salary ranges can be found on many Web sites and usually in the career center office at your college. And, yes, you can call your alma mater career center even after you have graduated.

Negotiating salary from the start is very important, because the salary you agree to today is the salary on which all your raises and bonuses will be based. If you take a lower salary than you need to now, it's probably going to take you much longer to catch up with others in similar positions. It also will sting when you realize two years down the line that you should be earning much more than you are, but your company can't swing another few thousand bucks a year at once for you.

Come up with reasons for a heftier salary than the one you are offered—and don't let those reasons be related to your major credit card debt you racked up when you moved into your new place. This has to do with you, your experience, and your potential. Know what you bring to the organization. Say, for example, you know another language. That can be useful, even if you're being hired for database entry. Do you have tech skills?

Some art background? Have you taken many public speaking classes? Any of these assets can be a skill at work, so think about how, and speak up about them.

Remember that your company only hires employees if needed, and the company obviously has the budget for another salary, or you wouldn't be sitting in the interview hot seat.

Kerry West,[1] 27, had to deal with confronting her boss for a raise. As a human resources employee for one and a half years at a San Francisco office of a major manufacturing company, Kerry realized that she could not comfortably keep living on the salary she was first offered when she took the job. Not only was it expensive to live in San Francisco, she also had taken on many additional responsibilities. She had covered for her boss for two or three months when she went on maternity leave, and the department continued to give her new duties. She even found herself doing manual labor on the production line when the factory workers went on strike for a while. She loved it—well, maybe except for the manual labor—and she loved the experience she got. But she also took on many more hours and felt that she should be getting paid for her added duties.

Kerry also knew that it would be easy to walk away and into a different job that paid much more. This all occurred during the dot-com boom in the late 1990s. She figured that she had the current economy on her side; her company probably wouldn't want to lose her just because of a lack of a raise.

So Kerry wrote a memo detailing accomplishments and explaining how she had saved the organization money by taking on extra jobs that took up so much time; the company could have hired a whole new employee to take care of the work she had

---

[1] Not her real last name.

taken on. She also had come up with several ways to save money as far as recruiting. Rather than demand a certain salary, she asked that her salary be reevaluated. Then she set up an appointment to see the vice president of her department. She left him the memo and said, "I'd appreciate it if you would look at my salary for an increase. Here's the write-up with my accomplishments."

Within one week, Kerry was earning more at the level she felt she deserved. And the vice president actually thanked *her*. (Hey, she's a great worker, and he was happy she pointed this out so that her angst about it didn't fester. The company wanted to keep her content. Try to remember that this is usually the case when you do a good job, and that will help you know that it's okay to ask for a raise or promotion when you think you've earned it.)

It's important to ask for a salary increase or to negotiate an offer, because your organization will likely see you in a better light than if you just took what they offered. Companies want employees who recognize their own value and are able to constructively negotiate . . . even those companies that really cannot give an increase.

Yes, you need a job. But don't beg for one. You're worth it, remember? Go into a negotiating session with a list of the benefits of hiring you, said Lisa Calla-Russ, a recruiter with Snelling Personnel Services in Northern Virginia. "Get off your knees. Stop begging for a job."

Megan works at a large real estate firm, doing graphics and the company newsletter. She has been an hourly employee since she was hired as a temp three years ago. But recently her hard work paid off. She was provided with a promotion that came with a larger base salary than she got as an hourly employee.

One problem: As an hourly employee, she got paid for over-time, which is something she has to do because of the demands of her job. As a salaried employee, she does not get paid for overtime. So she sat down to figure out the monetary difference between the two jobs. Ouch. Her promotion would land her $4,000 below what she had been getting.

She didn't know what to do next. She knew the company was tight on cash, and her department had even been told to cut down on spending. The holiday party was much less lavish than previous years, and there had been talk of layoffs. Finally, she convinced herself that it's better to speak up and let her supervisor know than to just let the salary issue go. She thought she might get bitter later on and knew that it would be much harder to catch up to the point she thought she deserved if she didn't bring it up now.

So she told her boss. She went in with the math she did and explained her situation, reemphasizing how grateful she was to get the promotion. Her boss was shocked. She had no idea that there was that much of a difference in the salary range and immediately took the issue to the human resource department. She came back with a few more thousand dollars for Megan.

If your company can't handle a monetary raise right now, there are some options you might want to consider. Think of some things that you might like in lieu of money, such as free training, an extra week or two of paid vacation time, a chance to go to a conference, or even a flexible schedule. Many managers are going to be much more able to negotiate these terms rather than hard dollars.

You also might want to consider negotiating for future raises based on certain goals you and your manager can set together. If you hit them, you get the raise and the company profits in the meantime.

But what if it doesn't go according to plan?

So you ask once. And if they say no, then it's time to pull out Plan B. Which really can come down to deciding whether or not to stick around. If you feel you are totally and completely grossly underpaid for what you do, and you were told there was no way the company could meet your salary or bonus requests, then you have to decide for yourself what to do next.

One thing is to start looking outside of the company for another opportunity. Even if you're not sure that you want to leave, looking for new opportunities will *not* hurt you. I swear. Ask around; maybe a friend or contact of another sort heard of a job opening that piques your interest. Check out the job ads in the newspaper and go ahead and apply if you're interested. Then if you get an offer, think about whether you want to go to your boss to see if this offer will make your company want to give you some more moolah.

But be ready for your boss to call your bluff. You really do have to go into the offer/counteroffer process knowing that your boss might say he's sorry, but the company just can't afford you and you should probably take the other job offer. Once that happens, there really isn't any turning back. You will have to go.

Really think about this process before you get started. If you honestly are not able to get a raise, or even soft benefits, like a few classes that your company will pay for, think about how important this job is to you. And think about how much potential there is if you decide to stay.

Is there growth potential that you might not get elsewhere? Meaning, if you stay a little bit longer, will you be able to move on from gofer to go-getter? Will you have some ability to move up and into the things that you would eventually like to do? If so, then maybe going elsewhere for a few thousand dollars more isn't worth it.

Do you like the people you work with, the boss, the feedback you get? Do you think you're learning more from these people than you might elsewhere? Again, then maybe a move for money isn't worth it.

Sure, we have needs. But remember, too, that these early years in our careers should be spent learning and should be at organizations where we think we're getting the best out of our working life that we can. If you feel you are being totally taken advantage of for a pittance of a paycheck, then perhaps it's time to move on. But if it is a choice between money and happiness, well, I think you can guess where I stand on that issue.

4

No Excuses

*H*e used to come into work late, complain that his boss didn't pay attention to him, and then say that he wished he could work on the cool projects. And he complained again and again to his coworkers, so much so that he was spending more time complaining than he was working. Maybe he thought that just because he was in his twenties, his boss should hold his hand and provide him with the good projects to work on. After getting fed up with listening to his whining all day, another twenty-something coworker told him that he should just tell the boss what it was that he wanted to do. And so he did. He told the boss that he wanted to work on X more than what he was currently doing. His boss's reply? "So why aren't you?"

Good question, boss. The fact is, he was making up excuses. He wanted to be put on the big projects, but he came up with lame reasons why he couldn't go out there and just do it, as the boss suggested: "I'm tired"; "My car is in the shop"; "I have a long commute"; "My supervisors don't help me out enough; they don't even know who I am."

Well, duh.

I've heard it all—from friends, from coworkers, from people I've interviewed, and yes, sadly, from my own mouth. Excuses are just that, excuses. They excuse you from doing what you really want to do. They excuse you from taking a chance and trying that new thing at work. They excuse you from excelling at what you already do. How frustrating is that? (Answer: Way.)

It's the people who don't make excuses and just assume that they have to and want to do what they are doing who get the extra chances and, eventually, the possibility to do work they want to do. They also get the attention from the boss. And once they start doing things sans excuses, they are handed more of the things that interest them, the exact opposite of what would happen to the person at the beginning of this section if he keeps on the way he is.

There are times when, in fact, you do have legit excuses—to some extent. But more often than not, these excuses can be turned into chances, or at least ignored while you go on about what you want to do. Take, for example, the excuse that you can't get a good project because you don't think your boss even knows who you are. That's an easy one. You go in and talk to him or her, explain what you want to do. Or you talk to your direct supervisor, or even start the project yourself if you're not stepping on anyone's toes, and line up a memo of the work you did so far and why you should work on it long term, for example. There are solutions to most roadblocks. The best thing you can do is say, well, that sucks, but here's how I'm going to finish this anyway. At some point you just have to realize that, this is the situation. Now, what am I going to do about it?

Another thing to remember about excuses: There may be a reason you keep using them. Does it mean you don't want to do what you're doing? Does it mean you want to get yourself let go, or you just would rather leave this company? Quite possible . . . don't overlook that factor. If you're not naturally a lazy person, or one who commonly makes up excuses, you need to wonder why you don't "just do it," as they say. The only people who really succeed and end up with a career they love are those who take chances and ignore excuses. If they listened to all of their excuses, they never would have taken those entry-level jobs to the next level. Or maybe they wouldn't have applied for that job that seemed to be just a little bit above their experience level.

THE MOTIVATING FACTOR

Hey, I'm the first to admit that focus sometimes gets lost.

Wait, what was I saying? Oh. Right.

It's summertime and you want to just be outside in the warm weather playing. Or you're about to go on vacation, and you only have days left until you take off for the sunny Caribbean (hey, a girl can dream, right?). But getting that focus back is pretty important, again, if you want to get out of a rut and get into the path that you desire.

As soon as you feel your energy waning and your motivation depleting, listen to that feeling. Then remind yourself how far you have come since the beginning of the project, or the job. That should help you remember that you can do something—you've already proven it to yourself. Each day before this, you did something to get to this point. Remember that and it will push you to wake up after a rest and get going again.

Sometimes, in fact, what we need is a rest. Whether it is a vacation that you needed after a long time at the office or a cheap thrill or two to shake it up a bit, listen to that as well. Going home to mope after a day of feeling directionless or lacking motivation is only going to feed that beast. Do something different tonight. Or go away for the weekend. Buy a new pair of socks. Whatever. Just listen to that need you have to change something.

> One thing that can feed a lack of motivation is a lack of planning. If you don't plot and plan a vacation, what do you have to look forward to? Nada. If you don't plot and plan, you're not going to have the impetus after a big project to go away or do something different. Even if you don't have much vacation time, try to take a Friday or a Monday off . . . or both. It won't seem like many days to your boss, but four days of no office land can really go a long way.

CHUTZPAH

Troy Farlow has some tales to tell. He has found his way to a great job, and he knows it. But part of the reason he is there is because of the awfulness of September 11, and he wants to make sure that anyone who knows his story knows that that awful day is part of the reason he is where he is today. But we'll get to that part of the story in a minute.

No matter what, Troy has a whole hell of a lot of chutzpah. Maybe even too much, he admits. Then again, naw . . . If everyone took their lives the extra mile he has, well, then everyone would be doing exactly what he or she believes they want to do. Troy has this thing—I call it determination—that if he gets something in his head he wants to do, there is really no excuse that will stop him. Let's take Troy's journey to earn an executive MBA as a perfect example. Read on, brave souls, and you may finally understand that what your parents always told you really is true: Anything is possible if you put your mind to it.

Troy graduated from Elon College in the mid-1990s. He admits that being the number-one student wasn't always his number-one goal. But he did graduate, with a degree in accounting. And with a GPA that was rather, eh. Despite that, one thing led to another, and by the time he was in his mid-twenties, he was working as a consultant at Pricewaterhouse-Coopers in the D.C. area. While he was there, he figured that it would probably do him some good to get an MBA. He conceded that this time he would take school a little more seriously, now that he knew what he cared about. The thing was, he really wanted to go to one of the best-ranked schools in the nation, and his transcripts from college probably wouldn't dictate that possibility. So, while working full-time, Troy took it upon himself to take a few classes at some local well-known colleges. He assumed that a good grade at his age from a top-notch school would do him well as he tried to get in to a top-notch school full-time. To begin, he decided to take a calculus course at Georgetown University. It was an intense (and expensive) class, taking up several hours every morning for a month.

Lucky for Troy, he got along well with his supervisor at Pricewaterhouse and told her his plan. He asked if it was possible to take the class, if he made sure to come in extra early and leave late and in general just make sure he got all of this work done. She permitted it, and he went to work. He would come into the office around 5:30 in the morning, check email, and take care of a few things before his 9 A.M. class. Then he'd run out of the office and attend class (a 30-minute drive away) until noon. Afterward he would slink back into the office and get back to work as if nothing happened.

It was a very tough class, but he survived and walked out of it (after some help from a tutor and extra hours outside of the office working hard on his assignments) with an A minus. But that wasn't enough to get into a great school, he thought, so he decided he would also take two econ classes (micro and macro) while working full-time. These would be taken at a local branch campus of the University of Virginia. Again, he worked long hours, worked hard, and got two A's.

Meanwhile, he heard from a friend who went to Duke University's executive MBA program. That person gave Troy a contact at the school—the director of admissions. Troy discovered the program's application deadline was only a week away, but he called the admissions contact anyway, in the hopes that she might be able to extend the deadline for him or at least give him advice about applying for next year. He and the director of admissions exchanged voice mails, and she finally left him a message saying she could set aside about 10 minutes for him the next morning for a telephone chat. He heard this message around 10 P.M. and quickly decided that a 10-minute phone conversation the next morning wasn't going to do him much good.

When Troy gets something like the following action in his mind (and it does happen to him astonishingly often), he goes through a process. For about five minutes, he tells himself he's crazy. For the next five minutes, he justifies the action he thinks he might take. Then for the next 10 minutes, he packs.

And that's what he did that fall night. He took a couple-hour nap, then went on the road from D.C. to Durham, N.C. Along the way, he left a voice mail message for the woman (from a pay phone on I-95) at Duke to say, "It's 2 A.M. I appreciate your offer to give me 10 minutes of your time. I apologize if I'm out of line here, but if we can change that 10 minutes of phone time to 10 minutes of face time, I'd be grateful. I'll see you in a few hours."

Troy got to the campus earlier than the 10 A.M. appointment but went to the office anyway and began to chat with the other women in the admissions office. He told a few of them his story, and they just couldn't get enough. They offered him coffee and a place to rest until his contact got to the office. When she arrived, she was a little shocked but handled the situation in stride. She explained that she had a phone call until 10 and then they could talk. Their chat didn't last 10 minutes as planned, however. It lasted several hours. Just like a date you don't expect to go well—then bam.

While in this meeting, Troy explained to the director his intense desire to go to Duke, what he loved about the business world, and why he was so interested in the Duke program itself. He explained what he liked about being a consultant. And he said to her that there was one major thing he needed her to know and suggested she sit down. (She was sort of waiting for a bomb to drop, he said.) That's when he said he graduated from Elon with a 2.5. She laughed and said they might be able to work something out. Then he said, "Good. Because I actually graduated with a 2.4."

This all happened before Troy had even taken the entrance exams necessary for graduate programs. However, she extended the deadline (businesses and executive MBA programs like people with some chutzpah) and sent him on his way with an extension of 15 days.

So Troy got back into his car and drove back to work. He had called his boss to ask if he could come in late that day. He knew he needed to bust his butt if he expected to get everything together before a two-week deadline. He skipped over the normal chain of command and went straight to the managing partner's office at the consultancy. This man didn't know Troy at all and was the kind of Oz person that no one ever dared to go near, at least not a twenty-something like Troy. Troy needed a letter of recommendation and a promise from his company that they would help pay the costs of tuition for the graduate program if he was accepted. Troy rightly thought he should just go to the top to start out. So he spoke with the partner's assistant and scheduled 10 minutes to talk the next day.

Troy walked into the partner's office the next day, told him who he was and that he had been inspired by this man since his first day on the job, when the managing partner had given a particular speech (which Troy reiterated). The man was impressed and waited to hear Troy out. He explained what he wanted to do and explained why this would be a good opportunity not only for himself but also for the company. Then he told the partner that he hoped he would write a letter of recommendation, along with the acknowledgment that the company provided partial tuition reimbursement at the time. Done.

This is a perfect example of that going-the-extra-mile cliché. Troy could have easily just asked his immediate supervisor for a letter, then gone through various channels to point out the company's tuition reimbursement policy. But he decided that with two weeks to go, he really needed an outstanding application packet, so he took his chance with one of the main partners at the company, a name that every person on Duke's deciding admission's team would recognize. This is not always necessary. In fact, it's not *usually* necessary. But in this case, Troy knew that a little extra pizzazz would be essential. There was that matter of the 2.4 after all.

Next came the GMATs. Ick. Troy hates these tests as much as I do, which really says something. So when his scores came back, he knew that they weren't up to par for acceptance. Again, he tracked down the admissions contact, who was visiting the D.C. area for a recruiting fair. He explained to her what happened and asked what to do. She got frustrated with him, saying that he had to give her something to work with. He left that night, mad at the world. But again, he turned that into something constructive.

He ran back to the office, penned a letter to her to say that the sum of his ability was not reflected in the scores and said if there was any other way to measure his aptitude quickly, he would do it. If not, he'd be glad to try again next year. With letter in hand, he ran to Dulles airport at 10 P.M. and knocked on the door for FedEx. They were closed; the planes were being loaded with FedEx packages. Troy, the ever-persuasive, begged, pleaded, and begged some more. FedEx took his letter, which landed on the director of admissions' desk the next morning.

Yet again, she was impressed. He didn't give her lame excuses, but he did agree with her and then showed initiative by writing a letter the same night that he saw her and getting it to her in the morning. Either it showed initiative or she just wanted to get him off her back. (I joke. That's not what a school like Duke would do.) Anyway, a few days later, a math professor ended up creating an eight-page exam for Troy. It was faxed to him. He had two hours to complete it and fax it back. He aced the test.

He found out two weeks later that he was accepted to the program.

I used several words here to describe Troy's actions: initiative, chutzpah, and gumption. (Well, I didn't use that last one, but his actions did show that.) And when a company, organization, or school is looking for a good candidate, those attributes are very necessary. Troy showed them that he knew what he wanted, and then he went for it, and with a bit more energy than someone who would quickly get a file together and send it to the school. Tactics such as these are not necessary to gain you entrance to a job or program in which you want to be a part. But the general philosophy here is essential in any good job, career, and life goal search.

"You've just got to go the extra mile," says Troy, who still goes to campus every other Friday for classes. "Call me a nut, but it got me into Duke, and it got me a job on Wall Street. There are thousands of people out there who want your job. So you have to show initiative and do the stuff that other people would not do. I'm sure at some point, it's overkill, but I'll take my chances."

DOING GOOD WORK, AND GETTING GOOD WORK FROM DOING GOOD

Immediately following the September 11 attacks, Troy and a friend, who had been in D.C. during the attack, wanted to do something to help. D.C. was all set as far as volunteers, so Troy and his friend hopped in a car and made their way to Manhattan's Red Cross station to see how they could help. They were turned away because too many volunteers showed up. Both headed back home. But Troy still had a nagging feeling that he wanted to do something.

So he went back to school, where he read a newspaper article in the *Wall Street Journal* late one night. It was a tragic story of a smallish investment banking firm, Sandler O'Neill & Partners, where almost all of the company's 100 employees perished in the World Trade Center. One partner had been out of town that day, and he was the only partner left, along with a very thinned out and devastated crew.

Troy had just been laid off from his consulting company, along with many others, so his time was relatively open. He had wanted to help, and this was where he saw a specific need. He took what money he had (a bit of unemployment and some severance), a suit and some shirts, and he hopped on the Greyhound to a friend's house in Philadelphia. The friend helped to get him to New York City, where Troy rented a room in a hostel for $30 a night. His first morning there, he donned his suit and walked to the building where he knew the firm was temporarily relocated.

He walked in and asked to speak to the partner, whose name he learned from the *Wall Street Journal* article. The person at the front desk summoned the partner and Troy introduced himself. He explained that he was completing an executive MBA program at Duke, had been a consultant but was laid off, and had some time to help out. He offered to do anything: answer phones, take out the trash, and clean the refrigerator. Whatever the company needed. He could last like this for a couple of weeks, he explained, and then he'd go back to his job search and school.

Troy knows that deep down, he also knew he would get some decent experience, being in the middle of the action, especially in a small firm trying to rebuild business. And he knew that there was a chance this could turn into a possible job, or at least a contact for a job later on. But when he walked into the building and saw the devastated employees, those thoughts were forgotten. "To help was my number-one reason for doing this, " Troy said.

After his quick pitch, the partner told Troy to come with him. He took Troy to a room where about 15 people were seated at their desks. "This is what's left of our investment banking group," he said. Then the partner pulled up a chair for Troy and told everyone in the room, "This is Troy. He's staying in a youth hostel. He wants to help out. Put him to work."

And so he began to work. Many of the employees spent those first days going to memorial services, so Troy spent a lot of time answering the phone, most often telling callers that the person they were looking for had died in the attack. He usually left again for the weekend, keeping up with classes, but he would return to do whatever the company needed.

At this point, Troy had a budget of about $10 a day. He would eat the catered lunch that came to the office everyday, and most dinners were spent eating two hotdogs in Times Square.

In the fourth week, with Troy's bank account down to about zero dollars and the company getting back into its regular routine, he decided it was probably time to move on. So he went into the partner's office before he left. "I felt like it was an appropriate time to bring things to an end. I said I hoped I helped in some way. Secondly, I told him I knew I had to get on down the road to a paying job. And he said, "What do you have in mind?"" Troy remembers. "I said, to tell you the truth, if you have opportunities here, I'd love it." And the partner told Troy whatever he wanted, it was his. So Troy said he had mergers and acquisitions background and would love to be part of the investment banking group.

All of a sudden, Troy found himself with a full-time job, and one that started out as a volunteer chance he felt he had to take. "I figured at first that the worst thing that could happen is I'd turn around and hop back on the Greyhound, no big deal. I figured there was about a 90 percent chance that was going to happen." But he knew he had to try, or he would have been left wondering "what if," just like he would have been with the program at Duke. Now, not only does he feel that he helped New York and the firm a little bit during the tragedy, but he also has a job in a firm that he respects more than any other firm where he would have acquired a job through the regular interviewing process.

5

The Boss Rules

*T*he boss: ever-feared, never understood, omnipresent, and omnipotent. That's what we grew up to believe about the person who is in charge of you. It ain't so. (Remember telling your big brother, "You're not the boss of me!" You were right. Carry that six-year-old's knowledge with you into the workplace.) Yes, your boss does have to say what you do and don't do with your job, but not your career. And if you want to do more than you're doing, make sure you do a good job with your duties and ask for that additional work you wanted to try.

There are some ground rules and things to think about as far as a relationship with your boss goes. And no, I don't mean *that* kind of relationship. That shouldn't exist at all. (I told you, we'll get to sex in the office later. Hold your horses. Jeez, kids these days.)

Your relationship with your own boss is probably the utmost important thing requiring your attention. He or she is the one who decides if you stay or go, if you get cool work or grunt work—and he or she is truly forming you for your future in the working world. At least, your boss's actions are.

No pressure.

The first thing you should do is make yourself understand why your boss is your boss, and what his or her job is. What is your boss's position at the company, what does he or she do day-to-day, and how do you fit into that?

Your boss has his own things to deal with, and his own boss to answer to. So understanding what, exactly, your boss is dealing with will help you understand your duties. How's that? Glad you asked. The more you know about your boss's schedule and what he needs to get done, the more you will know how you should schedule your own day, when you should stay out of the way, and when you should come into your boss's office to tell him what you're up to. (Now, stalking is not necessary, but awareness is.) Knowing what your boss does will also absolutely help you understand what you need to do and what he needs from you. If every day at noon he meets with the other senior vice president to discuss the week's activities, and one of your jobs is to keep him informed of the activities, now you know that you can type a little list for him to take along to the noon meeting. Get it?

Try to observe your boss as she goes about her day. Does she get stressed in the afternoon every Wednesday? Is she casual around the office, especially on Friday mornings? Understanding not only her job but also her personality and nuances will help you to work and improve yourself. You don't need to agree with everything she does, and you don't need to form yourself in her image, but understanding your boss, your boss's needs, and your boss's personality will give you a good base to go on before you ask your boss for a new project, higher salary, or even just some feedback. Which bring us to our next subject . . .

TALKING TO THE BIG KAHUNA

Ever feel like that person who rules your workplace world is sitting behind the great curtain and totally inaccessible? That may be somewhat true, but you have to face the fact that you need to communicate with your boss. We'll discuss in a minute what you should expect from your boss and what you should ask him about what is expected of you. But sometimes actually getting up the courage for any discussion with the person who holds the key to your paycheck and future in his office is a little intimidating. So how do you do it?

You may think that you need new duties or that your job isn't what it was made out to be. You might want to discuss a change you'd like to make or an idea you have. You might want a long weekend—this week. But, frankly, you're scared.

When you're relatively new to the workplace—especially a workplace where most of the employees are older and supposedly wiser than you—how do you get over the intimidation and stop being a wimp? How do you face that boss despite the fact you feel like a kid in a new school?

The best way to approach your boss without quaking in your boots is to prepare. Before you set up an appointment to see the Big One, do your research, figure out what it is you want to do, and think it through before you rush in there. Doing your homework before you talk with the boss is important, not only because you need to sound intelligent but also because it will help you feel less nervous about confronting her on whatever issue you need to discuss.

You also can run through your pitch or speech with a mentor or friend at the organization before you head in there. If a mentor has a bit more experience than you do, he might be able to tell you that it's better if you talk to the boss in the morning. Or that maybe you should wait until just after the third-quarter report. Or he may say that your idea is totally idiotic. Hey, it hurts, but it's worth it. (And, really, don't be scared. I'm sure he is not going to tell you your idea is idiotic. Really.) Oh, and another thing: At least you get credit for having an idea and speaking up. See how much you learned in the chapter before this? You go.

Once you know what you want to ask and say, make an appointment. Try not to just drop in if you think your talk will take longer than a few minutes. If you just drop in when you want to ask for something, you might catch the boss at a bad time, and you won't get a chance to go through the spiel you stayed up until 2 A.M. practicing.

It's also important that you go into the discussion with some confidence. Just because you're new to the workplace, or new to the organization, doesn't mean that you don't have a say in the happenings about the office. Don't go in with a defensive attitude. He doesn't have control over your life— you do. And talking to the boss when you need to proves that.

Make sure that when you do take part in a discussion and you bring up something you wanted to discuss, you don't apologize for doing so. That is a big issue with many twenty-somethings. They speak up but apologize for having an idea. "I think we need to do, um, X. Sorry." *Stop it!* You are a part of the organization, and your career development and job needs and desires count just as much as those of the middle manager that supervises you directly. Remember that. The more apologetic you sound, the more your boss is going to think you should be apologizing.

One thing Maddie Washington[1] wishes she had done at one of her previous jobs was to confront her own supervisor when she thought she was not given the tasks she had the experience for. "It's something I should have said much sooner than I did," she says. She's not alone. Most of us put off confrontation, even when we know it might result in our getting a better shot at work.

Maddie was told she would have a much more partnership-type role when she was hired for a public relations position at an Austin, Texas, technology company. That "partnership" term was even used in her interviews. But after a few weeks, she realized that she was much less of a partner and much more of a go-to girl for the daily minutiae, which would have been okay in her first or second job in public relations. However, that was not where she came from: She had previously headed up a community relations program at a large bookstore. "I was the one people called everyday," she says. She worked one-on-one with authors and large community groups and created programs and partnerships with the bookstore and its community. Going from a position of being the person in charge to being the person asked to take digital pictures of the employees at the tech company to put on the Web site was not what she had hoped for when she jumped onto the dot-com bandwagon.

When her supervisor asked her if she was happy, she pretty much just sat there, squirmed, and said yes. Finally, when she moved into a different department and began to work with a different supervisor, she confessed to her former boss that it was difficult doing the menial tasks she was asked to do and that it was not what she expected her job to be. Her former supervisor was none too happy to hear these issues several months

---

[1] Some of the names have been changed. This is not her real name.

later, and it caused even more friction. "I should have said something from the start," Maddie admits now.

ASKING FOR FEEDBACK

Feedback is your friend. Even if it hurts, you need to know how you're doing, what you're doing right, and what you're doing wrong. There are many bosses out there who forget that young employees (all employees, actually) need this feedback in order to improve and increase all the good stuff they have been doing. It's especially important to get feedback, because if you don't know what you're doing wrong, or what you're doing that annoys your boss, it's only going to decrease your standing . . . continually. Until you are a NOTHING! Okay, I exaggerate. Some.

There may be a way for you to ask your boss for regular reviews, or there are those particular few companies that already have a feedback or review session in place. But even those sessions are helpful only to a relative extent.

Don't be afraid to ask your boss on Monday if you and she can sit over a cup of tea on Wednesday to discuss your performance thus far. Make sure you schedule an appointment rather than just barge in and offer to see her after or before the busy work hours. You never know what your boss is in the midst of when you step through that door.

It's also important that you don't just walk into your chat with her and say, "So, how am I doing?" You need to come to this prepared yourself. Come with concerns, suggestions as to what you could do to help her out, and any problems you might have encountered thus far. The more specific you are, the more helpful your feedback from the boss will be.

Although getting feedback might make your skin crawl and your stomach churn, it really can be helpful both in the short and long run. In the short run, your boss will recognize you as someone who cares about performance, how you do on the job, and your career. It will also put it in your boss's head that you *do* care about your career development, so maybe she should care about your career development as well. And, of course, that feedback, whether it's criticism or not, is a good thing.

TAKING IT LIKE A (WO)MAN

The best thing you can do when you're getting feedback is listen, listen, listen. And if your boss tells you that you've done something well, bask (after work), but then remember to keep doing it, and more.

If your boss criticizes you on several points, which he probably will, listen to that and do something with that criticism. It's hard to hear, yes, but it's also great to hear. What if she never told you that your writing style was less than adequate? You wouldn't have taken up the effort to go take that writing class you asked him to pay for. Or if he mentions that you come in a little later than most, you can easily remedy that.

The worst things you can do are argue, get snippy, or blow her off. Then not only are you a poor writer, you also are negative and respond poorly to criticism.

Rachel Brown admits that taking criticism well is not her most stellar attribute. But she knows that she has to try, even when she doesn't necessarily agree with her critic. At her job, she and other new workers are given a formal feedback session about once a month. That was not an easy thing to get used to. "I'm not good with criticism, so the first couple times I kind of bit my tongue and smiled," she says. "But it took me a while to get that it is really helpful. Now I can take it for what it is."

The first manager to give her feedback was especially difficult to stomach. He pointed out several things to her, saying she did them incorrectly, when she felt that he had told her to do them that way in the first place. But Rachel decided to just listen to what he had to say, and the next time she was faced with the same task, she would do it in the way he suggested during her feedback session. "You can't take it personally. It's not personal. They're trying to help you and you have to accept it," she says. The best thing you can do is to learn from the criticism and move on, she finds. If need be, vent to someone who will understand and not hold your venting against you and not tell anyone what you said. Which means you might have to tell your dog. But vent away, because that sometimes is all you need to be able to turn around and start all over again.

Rachel vents to a very good friend who also started work around the same time. Her friend had the same feedback from the boss as Rachel did, so Rachel says it really helped to be able to talk it out together. "I'm not sure how many people can do that, but it did validate what I was feeling, and I didn't feel worthless."

FINDING YOUR YODA

I, for one, could never have made it through the first years of work—or any years—without mentors. But I'm going to call these people something different. You'll hear the term mentor used all the time. I think it makes that person sound a little too formal. Or it makes people like me feel like they need a person brought down from a Higher Being to take care of them. That's not what we all need. What we need is someone who will be our friend and confidante (to some extent . . . always be careful what you say to anyone when it relates to work). We need someone who appreciates us and recognizes our brilliance (or dimness with the urge to be brilliant) and desire to surge onward, despite the fact we are in a grunt job.

Think of this person as your own personal Yoda. This is a person who will guide you to choose wisely, young Jedi. He or she is someone who deems you important enough to put his or her neck out for you if the boss is deciding between you and the other grunt worker to take on that next dreamy project. This person is someone you cultivate a relationship with who will go to lunch with you when you need advice and guidance or just check up on you when things seem a bit rough.

Some companies have official mentor programs in place. They are nice to be a part of, and sometimes it's a great thing, to a certain level. "We have mentors out the wazoo," says Rachel Brown, the new employee at the large consulting company in Atlanta. But she wouldn't mind a few "unofficial" mentor types that she could choose because she has something in common with them, or because they have an interest in her . . . and not because they were assigned to be together. However, definitely take part in the program if you are offered to do so, because, as they say, every little bit helps, and you might even find a Yoda in that group of assigned mentors. But many times, this person doesn't know you yet, or your work, or what you're like. So their job is to listen to your questions and try to answer them. The best person to guide you, however, is someone with whom you cultivate a personal relationship yourself.

That way, this person knows you, has a reason to believe in you, and will *want* to be your champion.

It's sometimes difficult to find a mentor, but they are out there (and not just Out There, but probably somewhere in that vast land of cubicles). An easy way to find a potential Yoda is to talk to the person who used to have your job. It may take some time, but before you know it, you realize your own Yoda has been guiding you for some time.

I had many Yodas throughout my years, and still do. Some of them fought for me to get a job when I had no idea they were going to be willing to do so. Some wrote memos to higher-ups, expressing my abilities to fill a certain position I wanted. In my early days as a news aide who was usually chained to the desk, I had editors who would tell me it was time to take a walk with them to pick up a birthday cake for a colleague. Looking back on that, I feel those "walks" with an editor were spent on purpose to get me some air time, both real air and speaking air. Other reporters, when I was trying to write while I was a news aide, would pass me interesting stories to do and offered to read them before I sent my copy off to an editor. And some invited me along to press conferences—yes, to help them out, but also because they knew I was interested in an experience outside of phone answering. Some asked what I wanted to do with my life and offered suggestions. Others would simply compliment me if they saw I had a byline. I had editors who would spend time explaining why they changed things in stories, rather than just editing it and sending the story along. They provided a way for me to learn and expand my skills as I grew. Piece by piece, my

Yodas helped to guide me to a better job and a great beginning career. Many of them did it casually and probably didn't (and still don't) know how much help they were.

I'm not the only one, of course. Many of the people I spoke with for this book credit their Yodas as the key to getting in the door, or a promotion, or a new job. You'll notice that many of the people in these pages found their next best jobs, and paths to careers, through contacts and people who were willing to advise and guide them. Yodas are invaluable for growth, for development, and just for a little chat when you need one.

You don't necessarily need your Yoda to be a buddy or someone who will pal around with you outside of work. But you do need to find a person who knows you and knows what you do. A lot of times you don't have to be the proactive one. But as with any job promotion or move out of an entry-level job, the best way to accomplish a Yoda search is simply to work hard. Your boss, your supervisor, or the person who is a little higher up in the organization and sits next to you will notice the good work you do. Those people that you ask questions of—maybe that person you asked to read over your report before you sent it to your boss—are perfect potential Yodas. They know how hard you work, and they know that you want to get it right. What better people to help out than that?

This is much how Laura Green found her Yodas. As an employee at Watson Wyatt Worldwide, a workplace consulting company, Laura, 25, found herself working late hours and suddenly getting along with a few select people so much so that they would hang out every now and then after work. Or laugh at things while working on a project together. They were a bit

older, and she listened to their little pearls of wisdom and information about the unwritten rules at the company.

"For a while, I was, like, 'I need a mentor.' But I looked at the
relationships I formed and said I already have that kind of relationship," she said. It was not a mentor/mentee relationship, per
se, but more a friendship. She discovered there were people willing to push for her and help her to get new opportunities. How
did she form these great relationships? Naturally. "I don't think I
could have gone out and said 'Could you be my mentor?' and it
would have worked the same," she said. Rather, she realized that
it probably just happened when working on projects together.
You realize you have common goals and interests outside of work,
and then you begin to talk about life and what you want to do
with that life. This helps people know you and be your champion.

You may think that's easier said than done, but really, it's
easier done than said. Your Yoda will likely come out of a working relationship that you just take for granted. Piece by piece,
there will be that one person you know you can chat with
calmly and naturally. That person, if he or she is someone other
than a peer, can be a great help to you. You're not using them;
they are helping you. Accept it, and make sure that when you
do want help, you ask for it. There are going to be many people ready and willing to guide you and put a good word in for
you without too much prodding. You just have to be you and
realize who your friends are.

Heather Seigel's Yodas came in the shape of older workers
at her company who told her it was time to move on. She had
a few people she could easily talk to, whom she asked questions
of, and with whom she shared her work goals. From that, she
felt comfortable asking their opinion on various projects, ideas,

and even her résumé, when it was in fact time for her to find a bigger and better job. Her Yodas helped her tweak the résumé, find new contacts, and guide her to her next job.

SCREWING UP

Sometimes when we are in our first jobs we freak out when we make a mistake or goof up in some way. I say "we" because, well, it's all of us. (And it helps to remember that you're probably not the first person to call your boss by the wrong name in the first few weeks of work.)

The important thing about when you make a mistake is to make it, deal with it, and move on. Hard, I know. But necessary.

A Washington, D.C.–based book publicist told me how she screwed up big-time with an email encounter…oh wait, that would be several email encounters. There were two guys in her office named Mark. The 25-year-old publicist thought she was emailing the Mark she knew, who was her age, and whom she could joke with. She was brazen and a little flirty. It wasn't until later in the day when she walked past the *other* Mark's office, an older executive at the organization, that she realized she had been taunting him. Oops.

She decided to bite the bullet and go explain herself, because she was afraid if she just let it go, he might start thinking some bad things about her. When she told him that she thought she was joking around with a friend named Mark, and apologized profusely, he laughed. Lucky for her, he had a good sense of humor.

That wasn't the only time she goofed in a similar manner, but she has learned from her mistakes. "I would say confront your mistake right away. If you hide from it, you might give the person the wrong idea, or it might come back to haunt you in some way," she says.

Being new in the workplace can be a bit overwhelming and certainly stress inducing. It's no longer a world of roommates to run home to after a bad exam. We all have been there. So if you find yourself hiding in the bathroom, trying to stop the tears, deal with it, then get over it and move on.

Young workers "need to give themselves the luxury of making little mistakes and then letting them go," said Bruce Pomerantz, a licensed psychologist. If you don't, you won't enjoy your work, and you're not going to be able to accomplish much of anything.

You can expect that you're going to make some mistakes, especially when you're new. Explain that you're sorry you made the mistake, you hope to learn from it, and that you're ready to move onto the next thing, sans another similar screwup. It also might be a good time to ask for a mentor, if you have never been provided with one. Just say that perhaps you could learn from someone in your field that is willing to answer a few questions every now and then. If you do this, make sure your boss knows you're not lost, but you do think a little mentoring will be helpful. It shows you're proactive and truly interested in doing better.

Feelings only last for a short while, unless you keep feeding them with your thoughts. If you keep thinking how idiotic it was to make the mistake, it becomes counterproductive. By the end of the day, you might have convinced yourself that you're not worthy, that you will get fired, that your boss will hate you forever. Meanwhile, your boss has either forgotten the mistake or has even acknowledged that she did the same thing when she was new.

It's also very important to remember that you are going to be judged by how well you handle mistakes. Sure, it's not something your boss will write on your review. ("First makes a mistake, then goes out for ice cream.") But it will be noticed if you take that mistake, fix it, and move on. (That's the good way to do it.) Or if you pout, try to put the blame on someone else, or freeze because you're afraid to make another mistake. (That's the bad way to do it.)

Learn to let go of these things. You don't have to be perfect to be a good worker, and if you were, you wouldn't be normal. Mistakes are part of being human.

And if you make that big mistake? Ask someone to help you fix it. Asking questions and asking for advice after you screw up will only add up your positive points. You're taking responsibility and handling this with professionalism. That sends your score way up.

ASK, ASK, ASK

One thing that many young people forget or neglect to do is ask questions. You think that if you ask questions, or ask too many questions, you might look foolish, naïve, or just plain uncool. Untrue.

That is one thing Rachel Brown has found out since she started work in the summer of 2001. "In college, if you're one of the ones who asks a lot of questions, you're an idiot," she eloquently said. But if you don't ask questions at work, it has the opposite effect—you're an idiot. No one expects you to know everything yet. And, in fact, as Rachel has discovered, asking questions is looked upon pretty well. "Now, when you ask questions, it could save you a lot of trouble, and it makes you seem a lot more intelligent." Too true. She admits that a lot of times, at first, she didn't want to ask questions because she didn't want to look like "the stupid new kid." But she quickly found out that by not asking questions, she either ended up looking not so great to her superiors (Um, why did you do it that way??) or she ended up taking a lot longer on something that could have been a quick assignment, had she asked how the team usually handles it.

Asking intelligent questions also shows that you are engaged and that you care about your work and this project. It also shows that you get it (or that you're trying to get it). If you don't ask questions, your work will suffer. People assume that if you don't ask questions, you know what you're doing. Then all of a sudden, your work is all wrong, or you make a major mistake you could have avoided. So ask.

But how? If it's such a good thing to do, how do I ask questions if I can't, well, ask questions? First of all, know that you don't have to ask your boss every little thing that you wonder about. When Sue Schulz first moved to *Redbook*, it was her first real job, and she really didn't know what to do. Lucky for her, there were several other young women at the magazine who had jobs similar to hers. So she asked them how things worked and would run to them if she was stuck. If it was something major, like if she needed help with a writing project she was working on, that's when she asked the boss.

If you have little things to ask that can wait until the end of the day, or if you think you might be able to solve something small, then wait. You don't want to interrupt your supervisor 12 times a day. Now that Sue is a supervisor herself, she likes it when a younger employee comes in before he leaves and just says, "A few things came up today that I was wondering about. Do you have a minute to explain something?" When you do that, you're showing the boss that you're aware of what's going on, and you're respectful of her time. Clap, clap. (Not that this has anything to do with questions, but it's also a general good practice to pop your head in at the end of the night to let your boss know you're leaving. That way, if she has any questions about what was assigned to you today, you are Mr. or Ms. Prepared, and she's not left wondering.)

OFFICE ROMANCE

It starts with a little glance, a smile, and some chatter. Maybe a little email from her, asking how you were ever able to stand that long meeting. Sweet and cute.

Or maybe you're at a work happy hour, and that guy who sits near you keeps dancing your way, buying you beers, asking if you want another. What happens if you hook up and then you have to (gulp) face each other at work on Monday?

And then there's the older guy, who actually calls you at home to ask you out directly. Is this what you were warned about? What if you say no? Will that keep him from giving you the big projects?

Let's start with probably the most common situation. Claire Boyer[2] was a nurse at a hospital in a large metropolitan city. Bright, independent, and strong willed by every definition, this newly graduated twenty-something soon caught the eye of a surgeon with the same qualities. Shall we call it TNT?

---

[2]This is not her real name.

Soon Claire and Kevin[3] began to grab a cup of coffee together on breaks. When she had an accident with a needle, he was there to make sure she was okay. And any break they had during their shifts, they just happened to "bump into" each other in the hallway for a break.

Soon enough, the two were joining each other at hospital barbecues and coworkers' parties. It was a fast and fiery relationship. Claire fell for him immediately, and hard. Problem was she and Kevin had to work together under very stressful and even life-threatening situations. And not only did they fall for each other hard, they also fell apart hard.

After an intense few-months' romance, things at the hospital got difficult. As much as Claire wanted to remain as professional as possible, with her head constantly in the ever-important nursing game, it was just not easy to do. (Yes, it's like the TV show *ER* come to life.) It's not like, as a nurse and surgeon, if they showed up and decided they couldn't work with each other, a project wouldn't get done and the company would lose money. But rather, the "company" could lose a life.

For the most part, companies don't ban intra-office dating, but jumping into work relationships, hookups, or even major flirtations can help people (like your boss or other coworkers, with whom you have to work) see you in a twisted light. You need to be so careful about your hormones in the office. Letting them run wild, at least obviously for all to see, can really throw a wrench in career plans you had. You may be taken less seriously, or you may, like Claire, feel that you're losing a grasp on a potentially powerful career.

---

[3]This is not his real name.

For many organizations today, coworker romance is just another part of the lengthening workday and open camaraderie, especially among smaller organizations. Some organizations almost encourage interoffice relationships and hold happy hours in the company kitchen or lobby, complete with alcohol provided by the organization.

But you, dear newish employee . . . you have to be careful. Yes, your office probably doesn't have a ban on intra-office dating, and that must mean intra-office hookups. But if you partake, that could mean intra-office trouble for you. It can affect your career and your reputation. As icky as it may seem, people do jump to conclusions. And if they see you as a player, or as a person who is more interested in the meat at the office, your attempts to get people to take you seriously may be for naught. As they say, rein in your emotions and, well, other things. Then if you want to run with it, go ahead, but make sure you know what you're doing. And that's hard with any relationship—work romance or not.

Many smart employees who do find their potential soul mate at work take it upon themselves to make the relationship as unobtrusive as possible and often go to great lengths to hide the fact that they are together until the relationship is cemented—or until they have an office holiday party to attend together.

Julie, 28, found her new husband at work. But they both wanted to be so careful about not letting anyone know, that some of their coworkers were shocked to get invitations to the wedding. The reason they decided to keep their relationship hush-hush was not because they were engaged in a torrid affair. But, rather, Bob was afraid that if they broke up, he'd look like a bad guy and be talked about. And Julie just didn't want people to think that was all there was to her. She was relatively new to the company when they first met, and she wanted to make sure people took her seriously and didn't view her as someone who thought of work as a great meeting place for potential babes. Which can be true, of course, but again, discretion is a good thing here.

Then one day, Julie's boss called her in for an annual review. In the meeting, her boss said, "By the way, I heard you are dating Bob." Julie turned bright red and blurted out, "Am I in trouble?!" Her boss laughed. No, Julie wasn't in trouble. In fact, her boss appreciated that she and Bob kept it so quiet. It showed that they remained professional, and when at work, work was their number-one priority. Ends up the company threw an engagement party for them.

But not everyone is so smart about a new love interest. Take this one as an example of what not to do. In one small nonprofit organization, a new male employee came on board and immediately fell infatuated with the company's young, pretty, and, um, *married* office manager. He and the office manager didn't hold back. The situation revealed itself pretty early on, and it was very obvious to everyone in the company. It made office morale plummet. "People would come in and ask if they were married. It was so depressing," said one woman who worked with the two. On top of making everyone in the small office uncomfortable, the man was so distracted at work that his manager actually sent him home to work on large projects. "He did fine work once he was away from her," his former manager said. Acting in the way he did certainly helped the manager and his coworkers pass judgment on him. They got upset that he didn't carry his weight at the organization and didn't take the work seriously. Letters of recommendation and good words of this man to potential employers would be hard for him to find.

And then think about the situation (I've seen them all) when you start dating someone at work and break up. Or never really get the relationship off the ground, and then you see him hanging out with another woman from your office. How will that feel when you try to get your head back into the game? There are so many potentials here for screwing up; I can't reiterate enough how important it is to be careful when you're fishing in the company pond.

Of course, it's not always up to you, entirely. There will probably be those times when someone older, and not necessarily wiser, asks you out. But he or she might just be one of those people who if you say no thanks to, you feel like you're burning bridges. Maybe he is a manager in a department for which you would like to work, or he has the boss's ear, so to speak. Well, dudes, burn away. That whole "sleep your way to the top" cliché? Let it die. Going out with someone because you fear what not going out with him or her might do to your relationship just isn't going to be a good thing. Do what you can to stave him or her off, take whatever you have in you to resist, and if their badgering for a date or something else persists, go talk to someone you trust or to a human resources official at your company.

No doubt, workplace relationships do work out many times. But the best way to let them work out is to be careful. Think before you act, and think about your consequences. I know; it's something mom always told you. But when work and your career are involved, you need to set some ground rules for yourself and tread lightly.

6

Where Do I Go from Here?

*O*kay, so you've dealt with your first or second entry-level job and you're ready for more, bigger, better. You're even hoping to do no more phone answering. But how do you move on now? And how do you find that path?

Here you are, maybe a few years after you found that first or second decent job that provided you with a paycheck and some decent benefits. But now, you suddenly realize that's all you have—a job with decent benefits. Your perspective is a little different now, and you want a career rather than a job. And, oh forgive, you want to love it. You can actually do something that you enjoy and make money doing it. But how?

Sometimes sitting in a job that isn't the right fit seems like a complete waste of time. But it doesn't have to be. You can learn from your surroundings. One 24-year-old architect who works in New York City didn't know what to do when she graduated from Smith College. She was better off than many of us liberal arts majors; she had a degree in architecture. But she didn't have her master's degree, and she didn't think she could land a job at a firm without one. However, she wasn't sure if the first thing she wanted to do was head into graduate school. Groping for direction, she applied for jobs at consulting firms and investment banks. "Friends were investment bankers making a lot of money. So I wondered if this is what I wanted to be doing," she says. Turns out, it wasn't. "It just didn't seem right for me. Architecture is something creative—I would have gone from black to white."

In the midst of sifting through job offers from investment banks, she did land a job at an architecture firm. She still doesn't know what she wants to do, exactly, but in the meantime, she figured out that whatever she decides upon, she can use her time at the firm as good background. "There are still things I would love to do. Now I'm sure I'd want to incorporate these last few years into what I'm going to do next instead of starting all over."

A lot of people who are about to enter the workforce for the first time just want a job. That's fine for a time, but it means a lot of them don't do the preparation work necessary, like setting goals and figuring out what they want to do. So take a job that's not really your thing. That's okay. Now you have a little bit of work experience, and now you know what you don't want to do.

So before getting another résumé together and jumping into the first job offer that seems "fine," think about it. Do some self-assessment. Ask yourself if you think you will be happy doing this, what you wouldn't like about it, and if that outweighs all other things. The more self-assessment you do, the more able you're going to be to fall into a great new job, and eventually, a career.

Some people have suggested asking family and friends to think about you and what they could see you doing for a living. You might hear a common thread in all of their replies, something that perhaps you had not yet thought about and something that you could be interested in pursuing. Or keep a journal of workplace experiences. List what you like and what you loathe. Granted, many people won't need a journal to remember that they hate certain things about the workplace. But if you write it all down, again, you can look back and see a specific theme about things you want to find and things you want to avoid.

While you're out there finding yourself, don't just hide inside. Go out and network. Talk to people about their jobs, about their experiences. Ask them what they like and dislike about their jobs and careers. Structure it so you can be sure you'll talk to people; set a goal for yourself to talk to six people in the same industry this week. Consider taking a trial run on jobs that you think you might want to make into a career. As we'll talk about in the section on moonlighting in the next chapter, if you're interested in, say, social work, volunteer once a week to see if that is the sort of career you'd really like to dig into.

GOOD WORK = GOOD NETWORK

As with many industries, the magazine industry in New York definitely has a buzzing network around it. That is why it so helped Sue Schulz to work hard and work up from an entry-level job. In doing that, she met many people along the way and made a good reputation for herself. Although getting any job takes work, it can take a lot less work once you are respected and have made a few contacts.

While Sue worked at *Redbook magazine* for about eight months, the magazine's editor-in-chief became the editor-in-chief of *Good Housekeeping*. When that editor went to *Good House-*

keeping, she brought in another editor from *Entertainment Weekly*. It so happened that Sue worked for the *Entertainment Weekly* editor . . . so she asked Sue to come along.

Another great break—although I wouldn't necessarily call it a break. Had Sue not worked hard and shown an interest in the magazine industry, these editors certainly wouldn't have thought to ask her to join them.

When the new editor-in-chief took over, the magazine was short on writers, so almost immediately, Sue was able to start writing. It helped that both women knew her and knew her to be efficient, smart, and easy to work with. Sue was thrilled. Her first assignment, she remembers, was to interview and write about a flight attendant who had been on a hijacked plane. The attendant wasn't listed in any phone directories, so Sue tracked her down by calling the tax department. She found her address and sent her a telegram. Very exciting, Sue thought, especially when it worked out.

And although Sue's first story was heavily edited, she wasn't discouraged. "I was edited a lot, but not so much that I didn't recognize myself in the story," she says. So, along with her positive attitude, she was off and running.

She stayed with *Good Housekeeping* for about two years, where she worked for two different editors. Sue believes it is good to work for different people within one organization, because it provides you with different experiences, and it changes your experience while you're there so you don't get bored.

MAKING CONNECTIONS

You don't have to just network within your own organization. There are a ton of local business and networking organizations and events for you to check out. Listings are usually found in your office lobby, in the newspaper, online, and with alumni associations too.

Going to such events to listen to speakers and chat with others who have spent years in the industry, or who have been there just a short time like you and can commiserate, can be a perfect way to find new contacts and to hear a little bit more about this industry or job that you might want to turn into a career. Meeting other men and women who are in the same field can open great opportunities, even if those opportunities are no more than a contact list for the next time you want to move on.

These networking events can be held at restaurants, bars, or large conference centers. Some are very casual, like a good-time happy hour; others are more formal, in maybe a hotel conference room with speakers or panels. Some organizations sit attendees at tables to form smaller groups of people to talk about a specific topic—this is sometimes known as a round-table discussion.

Many people have sat in on networking events, started a conversation with their tablemate and found out about a great new job opening or discovered a different sort of job that sounds very interesting. They learned more about their industry or how other people have moved from one job to another to form a wonderful career. It can help you discover what you might love to do, even if you aren't so sure about this actual networking event or group holding it. Going to a networking party doesn't mean you have to be a part of an organization; it doesn't mean you have to be a part of the industry. But it does mean you can easily discover a few nuggets of information. If nothing else, it probably means you eat for free that night.

It's important, and can be easy, to chat with folks at networking events, even if you normally find it hard to break the ice. That's because these networking events are set up to do just that: network. Don't be afraid to ask people about their jobs, and don't be afraid to let people know what you're interested in, or what you hope to achieve at your company, and what you think you would like to do someday. Bring business cards along, or even a few résumés. Hand them to people, because they will ask for contact information. By saying what you hope to accomplish or what your goals are for the next year, you define yourself as something other than a go-fer.

Dan Sondhelm detests, hates, and despises networking events. He admits that he'd rather go to the dentist. Yet he goes to them quite often, and he is getting better. Dan is a financial marketer, so he needed to find clients, especially when he was so green to the field several years ago, after he earned his MBA. As a 24-year-old who had no experience, and no contacts, it was a frustrating and intimidating experience. But he swallowed his fears and trudged on. Part of the way he was able to do that was to remind himself that at least half of the people at the event also hated going. So to break the ice, he just asked questions. "People like to talk about themselves," he says. He didn't start off by trying to sell himself or his product. He just tried to meet people so he could later call them, or so he would know someone the next time he had to come to one of these events.

People like when you show an interest in their job. They will be ultra-willing to serve you some large doses of advice. Drink it up and apply all you learn to your position. It's amazing what a little time, tenacity, and talk can do for young folks who are ready to take on the world.

"I think a lot of young workers will sit at their desk, and they'll do a good job there. But the only people who know them are the ones they interact with on a daily basis," Dan says. "If you go out there, you're meeting all new people, so there's a chance for advancement, a new career track, education. There are a lot of benefits. And also it just breaks up the monotony of sitting in the office all day."

If you go to just one event, you may be surprised by what you find. They all aren't stodgy old things filled with executives. There are parties held at bars, there are organizations that invite young women to come to dinner at accomplished women's houses, and there are the more traditional eat-and-meet venues.

Remember Hillarie Fogel? She got several jobs through people she met at local networking events. She admits that, at first, she went to them with friends to grab a glass of wine and some free food. Hey, you're in your twenties . . . we all know what it's like to try to make rent and eat at the same time. So free food, free advice. And if you hate it, run far, far away. But at least you tried.

Hillarie so believes in networking that she now, in fact, is the president of Washington Women in Public Relations, a large organization that holds many networking events. It has already provided her with good talking points at interviews, and she believes being a part of (and president of) that organization has made her résumé stand out from the stack of many other résumés.

BUILDING BRIDGES

Darren Streiler, 25, has a dream. He wants to retire at 40. Of course, that's not always easy, especially as we've seen so many start-ups and hot dot-coms flail and fail in recent years. But when you have a plan and think strategically, as Darren has, maybe that dream doesn't seem so unimaginable. Either way, Darren's experience has led him to places he wanted to go, but it wouldn't have taken him there if he didn't plan, strategize, and take a chance. Who knows if he'll retire at 40? By the sounds of it, he's on his way. His is a story of determination and really using those contacts to get where he wants to go.

Darren knew before he went to Boston College that he wanted to go into business. Perhaps that's because his dad got him interested in the stock market very early in life. He soon realized majoring in finance was right for him. He waited until the summer between his junior and senior year (right after he studied in New Zealand for a year) to do an internship. His job was as a clerk with the New York Stock Exchange, working directly on the floor of the stock exchange, which was "extremely exciting."

He looks back and knows that he took complete advantage of the internship, not necessarily because the job itself was a super-great brain test, but because he walked out of the job with many good contacts. He knew while he was there that it was very important that he not "jerk around. It's important that you get people to respect you. Work hard, be efficient. That's how I laid my foundation." The harder he worked, the better his contacts were when he left for school again. It's a lesson we all should take to heart, whether we're in an internship in college or at our first jobs after graduation. Even those little jobs, like Darren's (he had to enter stock picks into a database), are important. And how we deal with them (i.e., like big, smart professionals) can stay with us years down the road, when we're looking for a job. Read on.

Darren learned a little lesson in college. While he was in New Zealand, he missed out on some credits that he would have to make up during his senior year. So swamped as he was, he only (ha, only…I laugh) received a 3.2 grade point average. Because he wasn't at the absolute top of his class, he found that his résumés were immediately weeded out—by computer—at the top-ranking companies in the top jobs that he wanted. He knew his year abroad was way more important than focusing on some credits he could make up, and he'll never regret his decision to experience life the way he did. But it sure was frustrating when he felt he didn't even have a chance to explain himself. It was then, during his senior year, that he realized getting a good job that he wanted was almost all about relationships. That GPA mattered to some extent, but if he applied himself in other ways, it would not keep him from getting jobs at the top firms.

So at that point, he went scrounging. He dug up every old resource he could find. He went through his high school's alumni book and "called every single guy who lived in New York City with a finance job." Many of the folks he called blew him off (awww). But there were a few who were interested in helping him out and admired his persistence (or simply liked to help. There are a lot of those sorts of people out there, don't forget.) They then gave him some contact names and numbers. He remembered that one time, when he was in New York City for his internship, he met an older man at a bar who ended up handing Darren his business card. Darren found it, swallowed any fears or shyness lurking in him, and called the guy. "Any type of contact I could scrounge up, I used." The man got him in touch with a few people in New York that he could call and check with for job openings. Even though it didn't end up as a perfect hit for a job opening, it was helpful, and it spurred Darren on.

"Persistence" is the word Darren likes to use. It was persistence that got him his first job and persistence that got him to all the others since then. He expects it'll be persistence that gets him to early retirement as well.

One thing that stands out to him as a persistence turning point is senior year, spring break. While all his friends were running off to Florida for break, he took his list of contacts he had scrounged up, and the new contacts they got him in touch with, and he ran off to New York City. He rented a cheap hotel, then dressed as nice as a college kid can and started tracking down his contacts. He told them he just "happened" to be in the city and would love to chat with them if they had a few minutes. He, in fact, got a job offer that way, which he later turned down.

Darren's persistence in other avenues led him to a job at Salomon Smith Barney, the company he really wanted to get in with. His father's friend in St. Louis worked for the company, so Darren called and called and called, until his father's friend got him in touch with someone in New York. The contact was in a department Darren didn't really want, but he interviewed anyway and decided he could figure it all out once he got his foot in the door. And in the door he got. The company offered him a job the week of graduation. While he was at that job, he worked very hard and, again, like at the NYSE, made great relationships, including one with the department head.

After some time on the job, Darren spoke with the department head about a move into the other section he originally wanted to work for. His department didn't owe him anything, really, and leaving them would not necessarily be a good thing for the department itself. But Darren took a chance. He nicely explained it this way: I know how much you have done for me, and I really appreciate it. But while I was here, I've discovered what I would really like to do and where I would really like to work. Do you think I could get an interview with that person?

He explained why he wanted to move into the other department. Without much hesitation, the department head helped to get him an interview. The human resources person in that department was pretty impressed with Darren's, um, persistence, so that helped his cause as well.

What else helped his cause is yet another thing to note: He and the human resources official had something in common. Her husband went to Boston College, the same school as Darren. He made sure to chat with her a bit and find common ground—something that would serve him well in the future and served him well in the past. Anytime you have an interview, or even a lunch or quick meeting with someone who may help you at some point, it's a great asset to find some common ground so you can chat about more than just the job, and that way they remember you. You stand out in that pile of 390 résumés.

"Just that I got in the door impressed her, but to really carry on the conversation, you prove to them that you can talk to them, that you're a fun person, and you're someone they would like working for the firm," he says now.

So, let's look thus far at what Darren did. He scrounged for contacts and got them. Then he walked the streets in search of a job and got one. He took a job that he didn't necessarily want so he could be in the company he wanted. He worked hard so people would respect him and count on him. And he then used his contacts at his current department to help him get a job at the department he really wanted. Done, done, and done.

Once in his new job at Salomon, Darren was put on a rotational system, as many young employees at the company are. It was a great opportunity to check out different departments, different projects, and different management styles. It also got Darren in to talk with many different people in the organization, rather than just one team or group, providing him yet again with more contacts and more insight from varied folks who had advice and guidance for him. The rotation also really helped Darren narrow down his choices of industries that he would like to focus on in the future. From his first experiences, Darren has a few suggestions he learned along the way. First, expose yourself to as many people as possible. You develop more contacts that way. Then, make sure you work hard, no matter what you're asked to do. Those contacts you make will remember that.

By rotating throughout several departments, Darren discovered that the Internet group was both the rising star of the industries he would like to cover as an analyst and also was the group that piqued his interest the most. Once he was placed in the Internet slot, he went at it full-force to prove himself. He was determined to work very hard and make himself invaluable to the group and to the department. Once he accomplished that, he convinced the group to hire him on full-time. He was 23 at this point.

It may be tough to find the same drive as Darren and others like him have, and you may not want to. But everyone has this gumption in them to varying degrees and to the degree of the job and life you want. Your twenties are an incredible time to try things out, experiment with different jobs and departments, and just go for it. Which is why this is the time to tap into your drive and not make up excuses as to why you shouldn't try something, or why you shouldn't work a few extra hours if you think it might help you in the long run. Taking a chance means you can't explain to yourself why you shouldn't try something. Taking a chance means you should try a little bit of everything, and work hard. You never know what job you do, or what person you meet, will help you with your dream in the future. Even—or should I say especially—if you don't yet know what that dream is.

So…back to Darren and the Internet. He got to the Internet group just as the hype was hyping and continuing to take off in utter craziness, grand leaps and bounds. He started to read about 19- and 20-year-olds who were making millions and going to retire at 25. That spawned a few ideas. First, the Internet looked to be the new and exciting ride to hop on. Maybe he should check that world out, instead of just analyzing it from the outside. And it also brought up another point: Retiring early was a grand idea.

"I thought New York City was where all the action was. Then I realized it was Silicon Valley." And Darren likes his action. So at that point, he began to talk to folks with contacts in Silicon Valley, and he began to develop those relationships.

Investment banks, he explains, work for the private companies that are about to go public. So he decided to talk to those people and get entrenched into what they do day–to–day. It ended up that one of his contacts in the investment bank went to work as the chief financial officer at a Silicon Valley start-up. And this man, with whom Darren had good contact, soon called him up to see if he would be interested in coming out to the Valley to work for the start-up.

One interesting thing to note: Before this CFO called Darren, he called Darren's boss. He knew Darren was interested in the Silicon Valley world, but really, what was he like as an employee? Darren's boss let the man know that Darren was a very diligent and hard worker. Thus the lesson: Even if you think you would rather do something else, even if you start to research what that something else will be, you still have to remember what you're doing right now, and you have to continue to work as hard as you would if you knew this was where you wanted to stay for the rest of your life. Your boss, your coworkers, and your clients can be the ones who build your reputation, or who will put in that extra kind word for you when you really need it—whether you know you need it at that time or not.

At this point, Darren had worked at Salomon for two years, so he knew he had put in enough time to gain a bit of a good reputation, and definitely to gain some great skills, before he set off for the other side of the country and a brand new kind of career and corporate culture.

He also points out that he figured two years was a perfect amount of time for a solid learning experience. But he knew if he wanted to go to the next level at Salomon, it would take much more time than it would to get to the next level after jumping to a new organization. Not to mention, when a person is hired for a new job, after receiving a few years in a training ground like Darren did, salary often jumps a few notches . . . not that we're all just looking for money. But for Darren, this was important. Remember, the guy wants to retire at 40. When he went to Silicon Valley, he doubled his salary.

He also made a huge jump as far as company culture goes. He went from the behemoth Salomon to a 30-person start-up firm. He knew the adjustment would be a bit of a shock, but he also knew that working at a smaller firm often increases your chance to try your hand at things you normally wouldn't have the opportunity to do at larger companies. So he was hired at a higher level, with more responsibility. It was a risk, but he knew this was the time to take that risk.

And then the economy turned, his start-up failed, and he walked right into a pretty bad time in the history of the job search. Hence, here comes that pesky persistence lesson again.

DARREN'S BIG NEW JOB SEARCH

So Darren took that chance, and, well, gee . . . chances come with risks. About a year into his new gig, Darren was handed a pink slip, along with just about everyone else. His start-up was sold and he was let go.

Picture it: Spring 2001, unemployed, and living in the very expensive Silicon Valley with the rest of the folks who were unemployed and living in the very expensive Silicon Valley. "All of my contacts out here were in dot-com space, and they weren't hiring," or they were looking for a job themselves, he said. It almost came to the point where persistence didn't matter anymore. Almost.

When Darren first discovered his company would be sold and his job seemed shaky at best, he began to litter job Web sites with his résumé. He soon realized that doing that really only made himself feel good. Without other aspects of a job search, simply posting a résumé isn't going to do much. It's not a bad thing to do, though. For one, it gets you started. It also forces you clean up your résumé, and it makes you discover the many, many different positions that are still out there waiting to be filled. But all Darren got out of it was three interview offers. Which seems like a lot, right? Well, he sent out 500 résumés at 30 different job sites.

To track his progress, and not forget where he sent what to, he kept a job search journal, writing down Web sites, job fairs, contacts, and places he sent his information. Soon, Darren learned how to be persistent to the best of his ability (which we all know by now is pretty big) with headhunters. He met with five to seven headhunters. Even though he knew he wanted to leave the Valley and move to San Francisco, he told the headhunters he wouldn't be picky and began to look at jobs an hour or more away from San Francisco. He met with headhunters all over the area and started to make nice with them. Most of those recruiters were about the same age as Darren, so they all seemed to have a lot in common. Again, like at Salomon, this helped him stand out in a stack of several hundred desperate résumés.

He knew he had exactly enough saved up to be able to last in the area for four months. After that, it was back to living at home with mom and dad in St. Louis. As much as we all love our parents, it's not a very fun thing to do when you're 25 and haven't lived at home for seven years.

Darren had walked right into an economy that "sucked," he says, especially on the West Coast, where the majority of dotcoms had crashed and burned. He was in some major competition, especially if he expected to hang around the West Coast, which he did hope to do. But for every one job, there were several hundred people like him waiting to join up. So again, it was a contact that saved him.

But this time, it took a little more than a quick call to a manager. It took some sweat, and as Darren is so good at, it took some strategizing.

He knew that even though he left Salomon, he still had contacts there who would be willing to help him. "You don't make enemies with these people if you leave," he explained. Many employers and coworkers completely understand if you leave and then call them again for advice, for consultation, or for—in Darren's case—help in finding a new job. Young people especially are expected to eventually leave a position, so many folks you meet along the way will not be bitter about your departure. Make sure, like Darren did, that you keep up with these people, and don't make the excuse that they are too busy to hear from you or too upset that you left. Get over it. If you did a good job for them, they want to see you grow and succeed. You may have to get in touch with several contacts to get one that is helpful, but they are out there. Suck it up and get in touch with them.

One of Darren's thoughts was to get in touch with a "very high up" woman he knew of at Salomon, who worked with biotechnology companies. He knew because she was busy and because he had very slight contact with her that he shouldn't call her directly. But he also knew that she probably had some great contacts in the area for him. What to do . . . what to do . . .

What he did was call a former colleague of his who worked with this woman. His colleague agreed, after some prodding, to ask the woman if she would discuss the situation with Darren. "I said, 'Is there any way to please mention something to your boss, see if she knows anyone out here?'"

So Darren's friend called him back and said her boss was willing to talk to him. She passed the woman's cell phone number along to Darren. It took him a while to get in touch with her, but he finally caught her on the phone "and it was amazing." Not only did she have a contact for him in San Francisco, she also asked him if he was interested in Denver or New York, because she had contacts there as well.

He nixed the idea of New York or Denver and told her he really wanted to be in San Francisco. So she called her contact and mentioned Darren. "That way, I knew I had the okay to call this other woman, who didn't know me from Adam." It also gave him instant credibility. He didn't just call the San Francisco contact out of the blue and mention the Salomon woman's name. She took the time out of her busy schedule to call her contact first. Don't be afraid to ask someone to do this for you. If they are willing to pass a contact along to you, they are probably willing (and want) to call the contact first.

The other woman ran a biotechnology investment advising company. She told Darren when he called her that because she didn't know his work, she'd like to come up with a project for him to do before she spent much time interviewing him. It took a couple weeks; he called, and she didn't return his calls, or she would return his call and say she was sorry but she had been so busy and she hadn't had time to give it much thought.

So he took it upon himself to come up with a project to do, and he did it. It took a week of all-nighters to finish it. (And you thought you were through with that!). He then called her back and said he knew she was thinking of giving him a project to do, but he also knew she was busy, so he came up with a project himself. In fact, part of the project included an analysis of a company he found out had invested in her company, so he surmised that would catch her interest.

Darren explained what he did and eventually presented the project to her. After a few rounds of interviews and meet-and-greets with people in the company, he was hired—with a 75 percent increase in pay over his last job.

Had Darren not come up with a project himself, he may have missed out on a great opportunity. It's easy for young employees or employees-to-be to get lost in the world of job searching. It's easy for employers to ignore or overlook someone like you, a perfectly fine candidate. That is why it's so important to make sure they know who you are. Make sure they know you really want this job, and make sure you're nice to everyone along the way. You have to do things to stand out. One friend told me recently that after interviewing about 10 people for the same job, the one that stood out in her mind afterward was the one who sent a thank-you note. "It may sound strange," she says, "but it really struck me." If you want something, you can't expect it to just come to you. Even those people we envy who do seem to have everything fall into their laps (movie stars, rock mavens, that guy who sat next to you in anthro . . .) had to do something—probably something difficult—to get to where they are.

Six months into his new job, Darren the hard worker was told that the woman who hired him was starting a new business. She asked him if he would like to join with her. The company was launched a few months later, and Darren was the first person she hired...and she doubled his salary. In those first six months with the woman, Darren said "I busted my ass, did good work, and proved to her that I was someone who was going to be a great partner for her."

Every job he has had to this point has had a common thread to it that he could transfer over to the next job, the next position. He knows that he loves to be in finance, and it shows. Especially as he chats from his new office, with the huge windows that overlook the San Francisco Bay.

7

Give It a Chance

*W*hen you're first starting out, it might feel like you have an entire world of jobs to choose from—which may be true, sort of. But you also must remember that little jewels of jobs, and hints of a career-to-be, are tucked away in organizations that you don't necessarily dig.

After Sue Schulz had done her poster of dog breeds for *Entertainment Weekly*, she started to feel like maybe she could move forward a bit. That's when she heard from a woman she worked with; another woman who had gone on to *Redbook magazine* was in search of an assistant. At first, hip Sue was a bit wary. She likes to put it another way.

"I was so snotty about it! I didn't know where I wanted to work, but it wasn't at an old lady magazine." But the fact is, it was a national magazine, and she knew she could meet a lot of big-time editors. So she convinced herself to go in for an interview. While there, she realized the magazine wasn't so bad, and even thought that it wasn't so much an old lady magazine but more a married woman magazine. "I was kind of impressed with it."

She was hired to be an assistant to two editors and was really excited about the prospect. She wanted a job where she was making a decent paycheck, and where she was someone's personal assistant, which was a step up from sort of an everyone's assistant, like her position at *Entertainment Weekly*. She knew walking into the job that she wasn't hired to be a magazine writer, but she figured she would go into the job, keep her eyes and ears open, and see what happened. "Some of the girls there were, like, 'You don't even seem nervous.' But I was so ready to be working and have a job."

It ends up, of course, that position was somewhat of a windfall for Sue. She learned how to pitch celebrities, she took calls from publicists, and she learned to discern who really should talk to her boss and who was a small star trying to get into the magazine (i.e., someone her boss didn't have time to talk to). She had to learn how to be nice to people and determine what was a story.

For the most part, Sue's job was very administrative, but she didn't mind it because she got to see how the editors put the magazine together and what the procedures were. She didn't get much editing or reporting experience, but she did do some research for sidebars in the magazine. And need I say she made many great contacts in the industry.

It wasn't reporting, but it was essential, and those experiences build up to a general knowledge of the magazine industry. Now, several years later, she knows that those experiences, and working at *Redbook*, were a necessary, and fun, stepping-stone to get to where she is today.

Today, Sue is hiring her own assistants and interns. One thing that stands out to her about "bad" interns is that many of them "don't care about the process. They get positions and they are scattered and disorganized. They are doing their job, but forgetting there's a whole machine around them." In other words, she cringes at the many interns who come through the office like a hurricane; ready to take over and not pay attention to the fact that they need to learn to move forward in the industry.

DEALING WITH REJECTION

No need to face it, you probably already know it. There is going to be some rejection in your life. It definitely happens when you're looking for a job, but also when you're in a job. Sometimes that rejection can be so devastating that it's hard to feel like you're going to get over it. But most often, you can learn from rejection, no matter how much it stings at the time.

Laura Green was faced with that situation a year ago. She had always wanted to live abroad, especially after majoring in International Business and Marketing at Georgetown University. So her eye was on the golden egg as soon as she heard her company, a large consulting firm where she also interned during college, had a program where several select U.S. employees could go to work in an office abroad for a time.

Laura applied, and her boss told her that she got the position. Imagine her surprise when, a few days later, she had a Fed Ex package sitting on her desk. Inside was a form letter telling her that she, in fact, did not get the position. She was devastated, angry, and very, very frustrated. She immediately thought her time at the consulting firm was over . . . she was outta there.

"Honestly, my first reaction was 'I'm going to get out of here, I'm switching jobs. I don't need to put up with this,'" she recalls. "Then I kind of calmed down and stopped taking it so personally and talked to my boss more about why the decision had been made and what were my future opportunities at the company, and what other avenues should I be looking at." She had been there for two years and was 23 at the time.

She thought the move abroad was a sure thing, and frankly, she had never really been used to rejection. She's not sure why her boss told her that she got the job, unless he heard wrong or just misunderstood someone on the selection committee. So unlike many younger workers who are afraid to talk to their boss about an issue bugging them, Laura couldn't wait to get her hands on her boss and ream him out. Of course, she calmed down a bit (good thing her boss happened to be out the day she discovered she wasn't accepted), but she still confronted him, asking why she wasn't selected and expressing her disappointment and frustration. Thinking back, she says, "I got used to not getting rejected. I got into college early and had a good life of not a lot of rejections."

So the sting stung for a while, but her conversation with her boss proved very useful. First, it cleared the air between Laura and her boss. Then, it helped her boss understand why this all was important to her. It also helped her boss think of things that Laura might be able to do that would keep her happy and be a step up from the work she was doing. Sort of a consolation prize, but more than that, her boss understood her a bit more. It's important to take rejection as it comes but try to move on and look for a good opportunity that may stem from that rejection. It's that whole thing mom always told you about—making lemonade out of lemons.

And that's exactly what happened. So as with many situations we all have to face, Laura just dealt with it. First of all, she convinced herself that now might not be the best time to live abroad. Her best friend was getting married, and family and friends that she loved were close by. That's a good thing, for now at least, she reasoned.

Then, because she was so upset at how the process was handled, she put together a note and scheduled an appointment to see the vice president of human resources so she could explain why this was a bad situation for her and how they can improve it for young workers in the future. Not only was she upset that she did not get in, especially because the company said it was a great program for younger employees, but she was also upset that she was told she got it and then didn't. She wrote about the things she thought the company was doing that went against its values. "I felt like the company made a lot of mistakes and was doing something it wouldn't want to happen to me or another person," she explained. This might not work for many employees, but Laura knew her company was open for discussion on employee relations issues. It helped her deal with her rejection to know that something might be done about the process, which had made the rejection all that much more painful. And, of course, she also dealt with it by going out with friends and complaining to them.

And while we're on the subject, keep in mind that venting should be done carefully with folks who work at the same company, which is what she did. Make sure the people you bitch about work to are trustworthy and won't spread your words around, or that they won't hold your complaints against you. You usually know who the best person to chat with is. It's much less dangerous that way, and you can blow off steam to more than just your Tae-Bo teacher.

Of course, the best thing Laura did to help her get over the rejection, or at least turn it into lemonade, was to talk to her boss. She asked him, after her big rejection, just how much growth potential there was for her at the company, and expressed the already obvious: She really wanted to do some international work . . . how possible would that be?

Her boss, who felt incredibly bad that he told her she got the job when in fact she hadn't, knew how much she wanted to work abroad. "I think I was in a fairly lucky position where I had done good work; they considered me a valuable employee, so he was more concerned about how [the rejection] would affect me. That was kind of a luxury that not all people have," she says.

Her boss came up with the idea that if she wasn't able to live abroad for a couple years, she should meet with more people here who have worked abroad and then meet with the international people in the international offices. So, she was able to go on a case-by-case basis to do work in the UK. She interviewed the senior marketing and account management people in their partners' headquarters and put together a report on the differences at the UK office and the things that office did that might work well in D.C.

"It was a nice way to give me a flavor internationally, and it gave me something productive to do," she says. Good deal for Laura and good deal for her company.

It's important that when you are rejected, you get back into the game. If you get rejected for something, try to ask why that happened and what you could do to put yourself in a better position for next time. Obviously, when you're rejected for a date, it's not always slick to do the same, but it's different in the workplace. Remember, you're learning. And sometimes the way you learn can be painful, but it's a lesson just the same. You can take it and let it help you build your own business, or find a better job, or like Laura, get a better position than you have now, even if it's not the one you were hoping for.

Many twenty-somethings are walking around with a sort of imposter's syndrome, feeling like they are mere school kids and their boss is going to figure them out pretty soon. So when a bad review comes along, it's easy to blow it into monstrous proportions (e.g., They hate me, I suck at this, I'm going to get fired).

> Everyone who has been in the workplace for more than a month probably knows some level of rejection. It's important to realize that you need to look at rejection as a way to change things, a sort of wake-up call about something you might not be doing as well as you could. Just remember, if someone didn't point it out, you could be just looked upon as a bad worker, rather than as someone who improved.

It's important not to wallow in self-pity. If you didn't get that promotion you wanted and you pout or announce you're about to quit, the boss is only going to be very grateful that she didn't give you that promotion after all. When you're mad about a rejection like being passed over for a promotion, try to calm down, and if you can, take a walk, get a cup of coffee. (Um, never mind. Herbal tea in this case. Definitely herbal tea.) If you get a whiff of irrationality coming on, do what Laura did and take a break for a minute. Think about what you're going to do, and what you can get out of this situation. Do as much thinking about a new opportunity that can come out of this as you can, so when you go to the boss and suggest these things, you show her that you understand business is business, and you're willing to put in the time and effort. She'll be much more likely to welcome your suggestions for the next best thing.

STICKING IT OUT

Laura Green was ready to walk out the door when she was rejected from the work abroad program. "My first reaction was I'm going to get out of here," she had said. But she didn't. Instead of running at the first sign of rejection, she sat down with her supervisor and told him that even though she didn't get that specific opportunity, she would like other opportunities at the company if they were open to her. She asked him straight out if there was going to be any growth possibilities for her at the organization. In fact, there were. Her boss did not want her to leave the company, and he found her work in the first two years of the company to be very competent. So he sat down with her to figure out a strategy, talk about what she wanted to do, and give her ways to get to those goals.

Sometimes when you want to run, it's not always the best thing. Frustrating that there's no one straight answer, isn't it? The thing is, each situation is different, and each person and person's goals and limit level are different. So you have to take the knowledge you have learned about yourself, and your company or organization, and do some thinking.

But what Laura did was very smart. Instead of wallowing in her own self-pity, and instead of running away, she knew that hers was a good company, and she thought that she should check out her in-house options before she ran off to join the circus or just another company that would possibly be a worse fit.

As Laura began her new stint as a part-time jet-setter, she realized that rejection is just part of the big life picture. And as the old saying goes, when a door closes, open a window. Or something like that. Along the way, in her new position, Laura met up with and started working with some great people that became her champions. They thought of her when good opportunities came up and were always willing to put in a good word if she wanted to work on a project or try something new. And soon enough, another big opportunity came along. She saw a job posting for a position in the company's San Francisco office. So if she can't live across the world, how about a job across the country?

Laura inquired about the position with the woman on the West Coast who posted the job, and because the woman was interested, she told Laura to talk to her boss before she applied. Although Laura's boss showed a little resignation at her newest venture, being that she just applied to live and work abroad a few months earlier, he understood the attraction of San Francisco and moving out of a city she had been in for several years. He backed her up, gave a good recommendation, and shook her hand as she walked out the door. It helped that he knew she was still in the same company.

There are many opportunities out there, and not all of them come in the form of a completely different company or organization. Laura found a great chance to work for a company she knew she liked, but in a different position and in a different city. Makes the adventure seem more adventuresome, yes?

When Matt Edwards, 29, took a job following college at a big consulting company, he thought it would be a good way to make some real money for a few years, then travel the world. Ends up, it was a good way to earn a living and enjoy a job.

After seven years, he was laid off in the big wave of layoffs of the technology bust. But his years from new employee to manager were filled with great experiences and great salary boosts and other perks along the way. He was so well liked that when he tried to quit once because he wanted to travel around Africa for a while, his boss didn't accept his resignation. Instead, the company let him go on leave, part of it paid, because they needed his new management and computer skills so badly. These weren't skills he had coming out of college. No way. He was a Spanish major from the University of Virginia. The new skills he gained were all taught to him at his consulting company. Granted, he joined the company in the mid-1990s, a perfect time to be starting out in the technology sector. But just the same, because he stayed on, he was able to grow, grow, grow. His contacts at the company also grew, and he continued to find new opportunities within the organization.

If he had quit and taken another job or opportunity, he likely would have been fine. But there are great deals to both sides of the situation. Had he left, he wouldn't have had the nest egg he was able to start to build after being at the company for seven years. Had he left, he wouldn't have made the contacts he made or learned the managerial and people skills he learned. It wasn't a lifelong dream for Matt to be an employee at a large management consulting firm. But it did allow him the time to figure out what his lifelong dreams were, and it helped him make a paycheck to afford those dreams to some extent. (We'll talk more about Matt in the next chapter.)

Just remember, if you don't like something, but you decide to stay for a while, it doesn't have to be forever. And if you stay in one company for a while and fear you'll never get out, or never be able to follow up on your dream of becoming a writer because you're currently employed as a computer programmer, it just ain't so. There is always time for change, and there is always an opportunity waiting to be discovered. Don't be afraid to stay at an organization you like, just be aware of what else you might want to do, and be aware of what opportunities are at the company you're in now. No need to move on if you don't want to, especially if you can grow where you are.

Say you like your company but your job leaves something to be desired, or you know that you're above the duties assigned to you. You don't have to leave the company to get the new experience you desire, even if you think there are no promotions coming up anytime soon. If you're not happy with your job, it's good to think about how you can reengineer that job at your own organization.

How? Take control of your situation. Make sure you've learned, and continue to learn, and that you've researched the company and your own job and what it entails. And definitely volunteer for new projects, or pitch your own ideas. In the meantime, talk to your supervisor about your goals here at this company and why you think you might need a change. Make sure before you speak with your manager, however, that you know what you want to do and you don't just ramble about things vaguely in the meeting. Communication in this situation, as in many, is very key.

Part of the issue here is figuring out what it is we really want to do, and why we don't just want to stay in the job we're in right now. That can be sometimes more than half the battle. It can take some time, and often, it can take some experiences before you know what you want next. Before you jump into another less-than-perfect situation, think. Ask yourself those same questions that should always be on your radar screen. What do I do well? What does my boss appreciate in my work? What makes my work different from those with the same job?

What can I do that will expand my experiences? What do I feel passionate about?

Of course, revamping your job is not an easy slide every time. If you expect to be able to go into your boss and say that you don't want to do grunt work anymore and you want to start doing something fun, it's obviously not going to work. You need to prepare first. After learning something about what it is you want to do, figure out how your change in that direction will help the company, and sell it as such. It's sort of like making up a business plan for yourself.

Once you figure that out as much as you can, then think about how you can do that at your own company. Perform well in the job you're in now, and your boss will probably be pretty open to you when you ask him if you can keep doing what you're doing, but also help with some of the speech writing, which is your real passion.

Twenty-five-year old Mary Keller[1] reengineered herself pretty successfully. After two years as a Peace Corps volunteer, she moved back to D.C. to find her niche and pay the bills. She landed a temporary job as an executive assistant with a D.C. investment firm. Not a bad situation, but not a job where she felt she could easily use the skills she gained in the Peace Corps and as an international relations major at American University.

She knew nothing about the business before going into the job, but figured if she kept asking questions, she would do fine. Piece by piece, she learned the flow of the place and did pretty well. Soon, she started to notice options other than secretarial positions that were open at the company. So she spoke with some people in another department and offered her services.

---

[1]This is not her real name.

She began to come into work early, before her secretarial duties started, so that she could work on other projects. After four months or so, she spoke to a human resource manager and said she saw a greater need in the department where she started to help with bigger projects. She also explained how that job was a better match for her own skills.

"I didn't feel I was being used to my greatest potential," she said. "So for all parties involved, it was a better fit."

MOVING UP IS HARD WORK

So once you do start to move up and out of that entry-level job, then what? For one thing, it's going to be a bit more difficult than that first or second job, and you might (in a twisted way) want those days of simple brainless tasks back.

Which takes us back to Sue Schulz's tale. After two years at *Good Housekeeping*, it was about time for Sue to move on again. Her next job came when a person she worked with at *Good Housekeeping* went on to be an associate editor at *YM magazine*. Sue followed, and the associate editor then moved into the editor-in-chief job that was vacated, and Sue became an associate editor. That job is where she learned the big stuff: How to edit, how to work on her own stories, and how to assign stories to writers.

As usual, Sue's hard work paid off, but not easily. As an associate editor, she found that level of the job to be a sort of make-it-or-break-it time. She was still just in her mid-twenties, and many other women her age were leaving the industry to head into other fields. It took long hours and a resilient ego to deal with the pressure of being in charge of something that ended up in print for millions to read.

"It was a really difficult time," Sue reflects. "You learn you either have to move up or out, and there are fewer and fewer positions as you move up." The process called for Sue to "wing it, do it, redo it, and then not understand why it wasn't quite right. It makes you doubt yourself." Many jobs can be like this once you hit a point just beyond entry level. And it's at this point where you pretty much decide whether you can wake up every day and deal with this, hopefully learning as you go so that it gets easier and more fun. Or you decide that the pressure and angst that something at this level causes you is too much, or just the wrong thing for your soul, and it may be time to branch off in that other direction. Each step you take in your career path can point you in another direction or lead you to a rather major decision. Sue's decision was that she wanted to wait it out. She felt like she was in boot camp where "they break 'em down to build 'em back up."

Then came the third turnaround of an editor-in-chief at the magazine. With that, Sue was promoted to a senior editor. "I almost didn't want to tell people. When I started, people were 35 and in the business for 10 years when they finally became senior editor." In a way, she felt like she didn't deserve the promotion or the title. Or at least she felt that others would look at her, and her young age, and feel that she didn't deserve the promotion. But instead of letting that get in her way, she kicked butt. Sometimes—and you may be surprised to hear this—some people at work get a bit catty about other people's accomplishments. But Sue just decided to deal with the situation, and if she did a good job, then bah to anyone who didn't believe in her. "Anyone who said I didn't deserve it, I was going to work my butt off so they could eat their words."

After three years at *YM*, one of which she was a senior editor, Sue did decide to make a break from the industry. She, like many others of her age, felt that she was missing out on the dot-com train and should try a hand at the excitement. So she quit *YM* and ran off to a dot-com that folded on her first day at work. (More on that little bump in a bit.)

After Sue found herself without a job, living in New York City, she started to do her own thing and freelanced. She calls it a good reality check. Among the many other things it taught her, she learned that she wanted back into the magazine world. Again, her reputation preceded her, and the editor-in-chief of *CosmoGirl* called to see if she would be interested in meeting. So Sue went into the office for what she thought would be an informal meeting. It ended up that there was a position open, and the editor asked if Sue would be interested in interviewing for it. She interviewed right then and there (which she says was good, because she didn't have time to get the usual interview jitters) and was offered the job about two weeks later.

LEARNING THE LAY OF THE LAND

Each new job, whether it is at the same company or not, takes some time to adjust to. Despite how prepared you are, how smart you are, or how cool your clothes are, you still need to go through a transition—that can sometimes be pretty difficult.

Our friend Sue went through many adjustments in her magazine worlds, but the hardest one was when she moved from her job as an assistant and sometimes writer at *Good Housekeeping* to associate editor at *YM magazine*. All of a sudden, she found herself in an entirely new situation. She wasn't surrounded by older, experienced editors. She couldn't fall back on someone else if she had a question. And she had to edit, which she really hadn't done before.

"I wish someone had told me that it was going to be this hard," she thought. "I remember being very apprehensive about it because I knew I was on my own for the first time. I didn't have those editors as my advocates. At the same time it was fun. It was a teen magazine. So I tried to have fun with it. You just went through it, and now look back and see you did adjust to it."

When she first went to *Redbook*, which she considers to be her first real job, she said the adjustment took a little less time than it did at *YM*. It helped that there were five other assistants just like her, and they helped each other out. "As soon as I worked at *Redbook*, it was kind of like the adjustment to the workplace wasn't so hard in terms of getting used to the corporate culture. I just kept quiet and tried to listen."

Keep quiet and try to listen. That's some pretty good advice. Seriously. One of the best ways to figure out how the organization works, and how you fit into that world, is to sit back and observe a bit. Of course, don't judge the entire place on what other workers at the organization say. You should form your own opinions. Sue said that when she first came to *YM*, she immediately knew she didn't have the wise editors, who had spent several decades in the field, on hand to guide her. Most of the reporters and editors at the new magazine were all pretty much her own age. So she wanted to be careful. "At *YM*, I was leery of learning the wrong things because everyone was so young. It was a lot of trial and error."

The jump to associate editor almost was too much for her to bear at first. She almost left magazines altogether. But she knew she loved the industry, so she just kept trying. And she's glad she did. The thing with editing, as with anything else, she says, is that you always get better.

But with that in mind, don't forget that you also can ask questions about the place, especially if the workers you are surrounded by do have a bunch more experience than you do. Then take their answers and advice and make sure to use your own observations to figure out what to do. Your own observations may overrule advice that you are given. But don't be afraid to ask. Like, duh, you say. Well come on, I forgot or was too timid to ask when I first got into the workplace or into a new job . . . why, wouldn't you be sometimes? I do remember asking if it was alright if copy aides could wear jeans. I was told yes, then I noticed no one else did. So I stayed away from my Levi's. This is where Sue's advice to keep quiet and listen really comes into play. Before you wear your most outrageous outfits, and feel like it's okay to barge into the conference room, observe the world you're in. Take some time to notice how things tick, and what the unwritten rules of your new environment are. Don't run into your new office, or your new job, and demand things immediately. Take some time to study the landscape.

Being able to adjust to new jobs and new tasks is a crucial skill in today's workplace. As you will find, the code you did this year will be obsolete soon. The Web site you design today will seem clunky tomorrow. And the peace you help bring to Albania on your recent nonprofit peacekeeping trip will have to be redone in a different way a few years hence. With almost any job out there right now, in today's changing world and changing economy, you're going to have to adjust all the time.

What Sue went through is pretty widespread in most fields. It doesn't just apply to the magazine world. You take a new job, and all of a sudden you find yourself without the mentors or advice-givers you had at your previous job. You don't know any-one, and you truly don't know how the gig works. It does take some time to adjust, but that's what you've got to give it: time.

If the new job doesn't match the picture you had in your head, that's fine. Accept that reality before you sit at your new cubicle: It's not going to be exactly as you expected. If you go in with a blank slate and say, "let's start," then you're going into the situation on its terms, not solely on your terms. Those come later. And if you come in on the organization's terms (to some extent), you will be able to absorb the situation so you can then move along on your terms.

On a bigger level than asking whether or not you can wear jeans, before you jump into the unknown, use the same advice to ask questions of coworkers on those larger issues that really can get you ahead. If, for instance, you have an idea but don't know how to pitch it yet, this is when you ask a new coworker of yours who has been around for a while. The people around you will likely be able to help you—or will at least tell you not to ask the boss on a Tuesday, which is his totally busy day.

WHEN LIFE GETS IN THE WAY OF WORK

Sometimes work just gets in the way of life. But what happens when that is turned around, and life gets in the way of work? We've all been there. Despite the really bad fight you had with your roommate, even though you just broke up with your girlfriend of two years, or following a phone call saying the bridesmaid dresses you ordered are lost in the mail, you still have to go to work and do a good job—especially if you're new to the workplace. Older workers often have the luxury of taking leave, or spending some personal time at home when they need to do so. But you are a little different. When we're new, we haven't even made a reputation for ourselves yet. We also haven't earned much vacation time. And we certainly can't ask for leave yet. But sometimes there is just no way around losing focus at work.

So how do you balance another major life task or event with work? And how do you not only balance it, but also avoid letting your work slip at what can be a very crucial time in your career?

People balance things in their own ways, and some days you might wish your Palm Pilot would just magically erase (and take care of) all the things you have to do. Alas, life is life, and figuring out that balance between work and life is something we do have to figure out for ourselves.

Cynthia, an account executive with a technology company, was two months away from walking down the aisle. Although she and her fiancé had a year and a half to plan the wedding, she was feeling the major wedding crunch time just as her industry's big trade show of the year was coming up. And she was a major player in the company's part of the show. Being the smart 25-year-old that she is, a few months beforehand, Cynthia didn't ignore that the trade show was coming up. She knew that she had to plan and prepare for each huge event so that she didn't end up in a big work- and wedding-induced train wreck. She planned ahead as much as she could, knowing that she would be stressing about both big occasions.

Cynthia tried to plan much of her wedding details in January, months before her summer wedding. She did so, knowing that work would really need her come April and May, because the trade show was at the beginning of June. She did what she could with the wedding earlier than most brides-to-be would have, so she could focus on the conference planning.

Of course, there are those little details that everyone talks about the month before the wedding. For that, Cynthia kept a wedding notebook in her bag. When she thought of something, she immediately wrote it down and then put the list away and went back to work, knowing that she would have the list of to-dos for her spare time right at her side. She has a 30-minute commute each way to and from the office, so she mentally sets that time aside to think about her personal issues.

She admits that there were times when she had to leave work to do a wedding-related errand. But she made sure to make up for it by eating lunch at her desk or working an extra hour or two later. She also made sure to check with the boss, not giving too many details ("Um, hi, my bridesmaid dresses are the wrong color. See you later"), but rather, asked if she could run out for about 45 minutes and make sure to make up the time later in the day.

Stretching out the day is a good option. Even if you're not much of a morning person, you might have to start your day a little earlier during crunch time. Sometimes that is the price you have to pay for taking on a life and work. Many workers who are trying to balance work and life during a specific event or time period learn how to get up early. That's what Holly Thomsen, a senior account executive with a public relations firm in Washington, D.C., did when she had to train for the 330-mile AIDS bike ride, a four-day bike trek from Raleigh, N.C., to Washington.

She started to get up and go for a ride at 5:30 A.M. a few months before the trek. When she wasn't able to get up at that ungodly hour, she would try to go for a ride after work before sunset. The problem was she never knew when she was going to get off of work, because some days are busier than others and she can't leave until everything is finished. So a lot of missed riding time was made up on weekends.

It helped, she said, that the office was very supportive. The company has a volunteer program where employees get five days of paid leave to do volunteer work, so she was able to use those days for the AIDS Ride.

Another woman, we'll call her Jane, works at a large human resource association. Jane says a flexible organization was the key to allowing her to take on both a wedding and the purchase of her first house, all around the same time. But she also had a demanding job. So she learned how to balance life's details during the past year, often doing things not related to eating at lunchtime, and if she had to leave early, she would ask the boss, with her own condition that she would come in early the next day.

There are several things to keep in mind when you have things going on, like these young women did. First of all, if you ask your boss for some time—other than earned vacation time—off, don't just ask for it without offering something. You need to meet the landlord for a meeting about your apartment at 9:00 A.M.? Ask your boss if it's possible, then add that you can log on to email from home and take care of some early-morning duties before the meeting. Make sure everything is covered before you run off to sign your lease in the middle of the day, and if your boss can email or call you on a cell phone, make sure to let him or her know, even if you don't think you'll be needed for that hour or two. It's also important to let your boss know what is going on—not the morbid details, of course.

But if you take a sick day to go wedding dress shopping and it gets back to your boss, it will obviously not reflect well on you. Instead, how about a simple, "I have some time built up to take off, and I've taken care of X for the day. Do you think I can take tomorrow off to finish up some details related to my wedding?" Then offer your contact information, along with a few extra hours you promise to put in for the company.

THE WOE-IS-ME EXCUSE

So, what if there is no reason for you to run out of the office, like a landlord appointment or an appearance you have to make in traffic court, but instead, you're in the office, but "out of it" because of a breakup? Or a bad situation with a roommate? When do you tell your boss that you are going through a breakup, or that your parents are getting divorced, or that your best friend is in the hospital? Do you make that situation clear to your boss so she doesn't think you're letting your work slip for no reason? And how do you handle personal problems so they don't get in the way of your trying to make a good impression and do good work?

It's not an easy situation, especially because many people in their twenties have a lot of new transitions going on outside of work that might have a big impact on the brain process. Deciding whom to tell and when to do it can be a little tricky, as can deciding what to disclose. The most important thing to remember, though, is that you need to take care of yourself, both at work and at home.

It would be nice if you could escape personal upheaval by drowning yourself in work. But the reality is, few people can focus on anything when something else big is going on. Speaking from experience, it's hard, sometimes impossible, to leave some issues from your private life behind you when you walk through the office door. Those issues often affect your productivity. So be careful how you handle it; your bosses may begin to wonder why they hired you.

If you think your problems are going to wreak havoc on your work, then you probably will feel an urge to tell a supervisor exactly what's going on so you don't look like a big loser. You want to unburden yourself, you want sympathy, you want to explain reasons for being distracted and less efficient than usual or than you'd like to be. But most of the time, your boss doesn't need to hear all of the gory details.

"If the problem from outside of work is not interfering with work, I would not disclose anything," said Bruce Pomerantz, a psychologist who specializes in issues related to home and work life. "If the problem is interfering, minimal disclosure."

The reasoning behind minimal disclosure is that you don't want to seem excessively weak or a potential liability to your office. You don't want your boss to think you can't handle that promotion you just asked for or that new project you expressed interest in.

And it can be an especially sticky situation if you are new to your job. It's a fine line . . . if you disclose too much, you may also appear naïve. Whew, a lot of things to think about when you're supposedly thinking about a personal situation. But you can't just let things at work slack when you're worrying about outside life issues. If you do, then you'll have more to worry about than those personal issues; work will be a problem as well.

On the other side, nondisclosure has its own hazards. You may simply be making a bad impression, and your boss does not know that you're going through some issues outside of the office, especially if you're new to the office. Your boss does not know if the slacking at work is your own personal lack of motivation or if it is the result of something else.

Sometimes the best thing to do is tell your boss in advance that you may be a little distracted by some home issues, and you are having some trouble doing all the work you usually do, but you hope to accomplish everything as you usually would. That is a better situation to find yourself in than telling your boss after you miss a deadline or screw up a project that "Well, see, I was having this problem, and . . . ."

When you're feeling stressed, upset, anxious, or depressed about troubles you just can't seem to kick away, and you can't focus, don't just sit there. Do something. There are always ways of handling problems like the ones I've mentioned. Make sure, first of all, that you're dealing with the problem outside of work, and not just ignoring it. If you ignore the issue, it will come back to haunt you and probably bleed into your workday.

Sometimes getting involved in activities outside of work will help allay your anxiety. Take on that gym membership full force, keep busy with an activity you like. And when at work (or not at work for that matter), surround yourself with upbeat and positive people, said Pomerantz. Try to steer clear of negative people who will only reinforce your current feelings that are keeping you from moving on. If things don't improve, consider seeking some professional help, perhaps through your organization's employee assistance program. You can find out about such programs, and how you can use them, through the human resource department or employee handbook.

The important thing here is to make sure not to just wing it and hope that things at work don't get too out of control. Your boss will remember when you screw up or that period when your head just wasn't in the game. That's especially important when you're new to the workplace, because the trust factor related to you, new employee, is still shaky and unsure.

So, if these issues seems like they will affect your work and you decide to mention it to the boss, make sure to have a plan and be professional about it. Tell your boss that this is your problem and you think it's going to have an impact on your work, but you wanted to give the boss a heads up and make sure he knows that you are taking care of it. And when you think the issue is wrapped up and you're back on track, go ahead and mention that to the boss, too. Let your boss know that you're ready to take on that next project you were excited about before all of this happened.

GIRLS (AND GUYS) JUST WANNA HAVE FUN

As important as you might find work to be right now, or right after you get your new big job, what is just as important is a good balance between life and work. Even if you like your job to the point where it doesn't feel like work (lucky soul), you need something outside of that cubicle wall. And you need time to do it. It's a tricky thing, trying to balance making your mark, figuring out what you want to do with your life, pleasing the boss, and pleasing yourself, having a social life, and staying fit and happy. But it's doable. And way necessary.

Why is it necessary, you ask? Because all work and no play . . . you know the cliché. But honestly, no play, no time to breathe, no time to yourself will only land you a dull spot. You won't be creative or energized to start anew, to explore and experience. Sure, you may be putting in the hours that the boss oh so appreciates . . . if he notices. But what are those hours adding up to?

Getting out of the office to actually use those tickets to see your favorite band can be tough if you're the youngest one in the office. Many workplaces will forget about the balance needs of those who don't have children or are a bit younger than the other workers. As companies today tout family-friendly policies (which, of course, are great), young workers may sometimes be put in the position of having to pick up the slack. Saying no is a tough thing, especially when it is backed up with guilt and a desire to get ahead.

It's easy to say yes, especially if you're the youngest person in the workplace. So how do you break the cycle and say no? You have to realize that you can.

A lot of people feel that if they don't have a family, they must stay late at the office, even if they aren't asked. This is because maybe they are the youngest one in the office, and they feel the need to stay late to prove themselves. The problem is, the managers don't always notice. So it's important to be up front with managers as much as you can. A simple "I really would love to stay late and help out tonight, but I did that twice last week. I am finished with my work, and I have important plans tonight" will do. There. Easy, right? Well, never really, but it is very important that you make sure you have that balance.

Sometimes when we're younger, we want to make a quick, fast start, said the woman who kept staying late for those who had families. But even young people need to sit back and take a breather or we'll be burnt out before we have a gray hair.

A young associate at a large law firm in D.C. faced the same issue. Large law firms in the area are notorious for working their young associates long hours. And this lawyer knew that. At 27, she was usually working 12 hours a day. Because she was single, she tended to feel guiltier about leaving at the end of the day than a family person would. So she tried to remind herself that she, too, had a personal life.

Although she was with the firm for only a year, she caught on quickly to more than just the legal profession. "If you don't take time for yourself, then you won't enjoy your work anymore," she said.

But workplace experts, managers, and others agree that it is important for young workers to be prudent about asking for more freedom. They say young workers need to remember they are the low rung on the ladder. So if you're asking to leave early (or even just on time), make sure you do so when things at your organization aren't the busiest. The young lawyer said she made sure not to leave early when in the middle of preparing for a big trial. It's also a good idea to make sure you've proven yourself as a hard worker before you ask for some personal time or to leave a few hours early.

Sometimes managers don't have a clue and often forget or don't realize how big of a toll work puts on a person's personal time. So it may help you to plan that time and really think ahead of schedule about when you're going to that concert. Make sure you get your work done before the show so you can slip out of the office at a decent hour. It's very important to make sure your manager knows you work hard and that you're willing to put in the extra hours. But it is equally important to let yourself have some hours outside of work. If you don't do that, you're going to resent work. Not a good thing if you're trying to figure it out and get ahead. And that resentment will show itself in your product and your attitude.

MOONLIGHTING

Ever feel like you can't make the rent? Okay, you really *can't* make the rent? It might be time to moonlight, rather than call the parents. They will be so pleased.

Moonlighting can serve two needs. You can find a second job to help pay off that credit card debt, or you can find a second job to help you figure out what you want to do. Not that we're here searching for ways to up the brownie points with the parents, but that reason will also please them ever so much. The other need it serves is the reason Nikki Anesi is moonlighting. Nikki might possibly want to be an entertainer of some sort someday . . . although she already is sometimes. Seems like stand-up comedy might be the leading candidate. I'm sure, however, that there are people in her life who are pleased the stand-up work comes in after her day job as an executive assistant at a large New York branding company (read: Mom and Dad).

Sometimes, obviously in the case of the latter, these second jobs are taken on not for the paycheck but more for the experience. Which can make you much richer than any job at a restaurant.

Taking a second job on top of the one you have now might seem like a bit too much for a twenty-something to juggle. And it might be. But there is the other side of the spectrum as well. Second jobs can be the thing that brings in the extra few hundred bucks a month to help you get through, get that new suit you need, or get some money in the bank, which is kind of a necessary thing. My after-college-years roommate gained several things during her stint as a moonlighter. She loved going to the gym, but the extra $75 a month it cost was just a bit much on our little twenty-something budgets. So she started to work at the gym a few hours every Sunday morning, collecting membership cards. Not only did she get a free membership, but she also got a few extra bucks in the meantime.

What I consider more important, though, is a second job that can help you figure out what you're interested in. Say you don't really dig that job at the consultancy and think you might be more interested in doing social work—the area you thought you might be interested in back when you were in college. How about trying to work twice a month at a local home for abused children? It will give you an opportunity to get a taste for that other thing you think you might like to do. It will also provide you with great resources in the form of other social workers, who can tell you what it's like, what they like about the job, what they don't like, and what they would have wished someone had told them before they took this on as a career.

Like Nikki, moonlighting can also help you get some balance in your life. You don't want to end up as a 9-to-5 working stiff, now do you? Throw some balance and excitement in that life of yours.

Long before she graduated and before she moved to New York, Nikki, 23, did improv work, acted, and was in the theater. She's a pretty funny woman, and her friends often told her so. They would tell her that a little monologue she just unknowingly entertained them with would make a great stand-up routine.

So when she got to New York, she figured why not give it a try? And she soon signed up for a stand-up class. The best thing the class did for her was help her hone some material and allow her stage time at a local comedy club. The students were intermingled with pros, so the audience couldn't tell who was new. Nikki was the last to go, and she was hooted and hollered (in a good way). She did such a bang-up job, the club owner asked her if she would be interested in a repeat performance.

"I've always had the entertainment bug in me," she explained. "And I like to have something else in my life. I'm not the kind of person who likes to work and then go home." As well as she has been received so far in this stand-up world, she isn't ready to give up her day job just yet. First of all, she really likes what she does. Second, she said she's not ready, nor does she have the willpower, to do the starving comic thing just yet. Or maybe ever. "I like to have things aside from the office. My job is very entertaining and I like what I do. But [moonlighting] is not like a getaway for me. It's more of a mindbender."

Not only does her stand-up life help her bend that mind of hers; it also provides insight into her future possibilities, and it provides a little paycheck every now and then, when she agrees to do an open mike night, like she did after the class she took. Wins all around.

So, say you want to go to law school, but you're not willing to give up your day job? It can be done, with a little squeezing here and there. One 25-year-old woman—we'll call her Jennifer Glenn—who wasn't willing to give up her day job as a recruiter did just that. Balancing a job as a recruiter and a new journey into law school ain't easy by any means. But it is important to her both to have a day job for experience and pay and to go to law school. So she helps herself a lot by making sure to keep the two projects very separate. She focuses on keeping school and work in their place. For instance, she would never consider closing her office door to study; that won't help her job, for sure, and it certainly won't help her focus on the law schoolwork. If she felt she could close the door and hit the books, she probably wouldn't get as much quality studying time done, she says. Hence, she makes sure to set aside enough time on nights and weekends to read and study for school. If she didn't, she would feel like she was cheating herself out of an education. In other words, she owes it to herself to sacrifice some free time on weekends so that she can focus on this new law school venture.

To be able to do two very different things in one 24-hour period, drawing up a detailed schedule is often necessary. But make sure to add in some free time or you will burn out.

Another young woman graduated with a degree in graphic arts but could not find a great job in her field. So she found something similar and landed a job as an information systems technician at a local arts co-op. It is a good job, and she is very tech savvy, but actually doing art is her number-one goal. So in addition to working hard at her day job, she spends time at the co-op painting and sculpting. Because she does so well as a technician, and works hard to boot, she was able to ask her boss for a flexible schedule so that her weekend is Sunday and Monday instead of the regular Saturday and Sunday weekend. That way, she is able to use her days off to touch base with potential clients and to tackle her own projects. She sells her paintings and sculptures on commission in places like Washington, D.C., and in New York. Until she knows she can support herself fully on art, she will keep her current job, where she excels.

Not all would-be artists are lucky enough to find a job at a gallery. One young woman, for instance, is a full-time staff engineer with a firm in Northern Virginia. She discovered her talent for painting a few years ago, and her hours after work and on weekends are increasingly spent on what was once a hobby, but what might one day be her career.

Balancing between her 10-hour workday and her true love has been tricky. She sets a goal for herself every day, even if it is something relatively small, such as updating her art contacts list. From that, she has been able to host shows and sell some of her work. She spends weekends painting or visiting potential clients, and also knows that her art alone will not support her right now. Balancing between her 10-hour workday and her true passion has been tricky, but so worth it.

By moonlighting, like these folks did, you can figure out if some seemingly far-off dream is attainable. And if you find that it is, then you can decide when it's time to quit that day job and go for a life of full-time stand-up comedy. Nikki said she is not willing to live that starving artist life just yet, or ever, probably. But if the stand-up routine were to take off and promise her a full-time comedy life like that of Jerry Seinfeld or Margaret Cho, for instance, she'd certainly hop on board, she said.

FREAK YOUR PARENTS OUT

This is a different generation from that of our parents. Many of our parents followed one path, stayed with one company, and would not have wanted to break the rules or start a dot-com at age 25. Work today is different.

I met a guy recently at a D.C. craft, food, and art market. His uncle, a photographer, was gone for the day, so this guy spent his Saturday selling his uncle's photographs.

Guy: "I help my uncle out. Wish I had a cooler title, but I just hold stuff."
Me: "You could call yourself the producer."
Guy: "Hey. Good idea."

Me: "Is this your full-time job?" (I can't help it. I ask everyone.)

Guy: "No. I'm in software," he said sheepishly. "I kind of wish I would get laid off."

That last statement did not surprise me whatsoever. So many of us twenty-somethings are part of a generation of folks who know there are many great experiences to be had. In Guy's case, he thought getting laid off would push him to travel with his uncle, help with photo shoots, and find something off the wall to do "for a little while at least."

Would our parents and those in their generation have wanted to be laid off? Not a chance. Even as we are faced with a recession right now (that may be changing as you read this book . . .), many of us acknowledge the fact that there is always going to be something else. Some sacrifices may have to be made between the something and the something else, but so many people are willing to deal with smaller paychecks if it means a little adventure is in store. Or a little excitement is around the corner.

Sometimes taking a break from work, or taking a chance, even though others might discourage you, is the best way to take a step toward your happy place.

No one said work—or life after college—was easy. In fact, that's kind of the point. This is a time to figure things out, to take a chance, and to do just the opposite of what the Safety Manual of Life would tell you to do. Sometimes the best path to a great career is not the one careful parents or practical advisors would tell you to take.

It's important to remember that you don't have to be number one from the start (and you won't be), and you don't have to know what you are going to do with your life from the beginning. Taking a chance on random jobs, or things that you want to do, is very important for your own development, career or otherwise.

Take Jonathan Kaplan, for example.

Here's a guy that most folks would kick for what he did. Well, at least at first. I personally think many people who know him respect what he did, and when I tell his story, my friends all gasp in awe. (And ask if he is married. He is.)

Jonathan was a twenty-something new, young man on an old, established block. He spent four years landing different jobs in the D.C. area that most would consider to be on the perfect path to a powerful career. He started out at the Progressive Policy Institute, then he worked for Congressman Ken Bensten (D-Tex.), and finally, he moved to the White House, where he helped write speeches and event briefings for Tipper Gore. All at an age when many are still interviewing for a job that consists of little more than stapling faxes.

But Jonathan wanted something more, and he got it: A lottery spot to compete in the Ironman Triathlon in Hawaii. It was an athlete's dream-come-true. But it was more than that. As Jonathan said, he felt he was in a spot in his career where the work was simply frustrating. "I wanted to do so much, and felt like I was doing so little," he says. The political world to him, he said, was a world of "hurry up and wait," where there was a lot of pressure, and then a lot of down time. That may not be the case in the higher-up positions, but he wasn't in that place yet, and he wasn't sure how long he wanted to stick around to possibly get to that place. It was during the down time that Jonathan had the itch to do something, anything. And as he sat there during down time, he felt tremendous guilt about not being busy.

So the Ironman ended up being another avenue for Jonathan, beyond just a great physical challenge. He knew he always wanted to write . . . more than Tipper's briefing book. He saw this triathlon as the perfect subject to pitch as a story for a magazine or newspaper. It would be his first big freelance article, which could give him some insight to another possible career for the future. But in the meantime, he was at the White House, and he wasn't sure that he was ready to completely let go of the political career he had started to build for himself.

The problem with the Ironman was that he knew he needed to take some time off to train. He "kept putting off the issue," afraid, and rightly so, that he wouldn't be permitted to take leave. So when he found out that any time off was not an option, he grabbed his thesaurus, Rolodex, and hit the road. But not before he made one little (ahem) mistake.

Oops. But not really . . .

Jonathan knew before he left his position at the White House that he wanted something more. Not only was the Tipper Gore job tough, demanding, and sometimes dull work, but Jonathan knew that there was something else out there for him. So when the chance opportunity came up for him to compete in the Ironman, he felt that was a once-in-a-lifetime opportunity, and it would make a great subject to write about.

After Jonathan decided to leave the White House so he could train and write, a mentor at the office, whom he really respected and trusted, told him it was a bad idea to just do the Ironman without a job waiting for him when he was finished. He basically told Jonathan that there was no real middle ground in the political world. You're either up there or down there, and if Jonathan wanted to ride his bike or run, then he should find another profession.

He said that it would be impossible to get back into the Washington political circle if he didn't clinch something before he left. Jonathan didn't want to do it, but he really took this man's word for gold and immediately followed up on an opening he heard about at the Democratic National Committee. In the interview at the DNC, Jonathan asked if he could have some time off to train. His interviewer said that wouldn't work, but they offered him the job. Jonathan took it, assuming he could finesse something later.

Jonathan reported to work July 5, just a few months before the October triathlon. He knew almost immediately that he had made a mistake. Not only was he sure he wouldn't be given time off, but he just didn't want to be there. He didn't like the atmosphere, and even if things at the office showed signs that they would perk up, he knew he still didn't want to be there. So Jonathan went to see a career counselor that night who helped him boost his confidence to go in the next day and just say no. He went to the office the following morning with the "what's the worst that could happen?" mantra in his head.

The worst pretty much did happen. Jonathan went to talk to his new boss outside, where he was taking a smoke break. He explained that he was very sorry, but he made a mistake. He said he wasn't mentally prepared for the job and really wanted to focus on the Ironman. And, simply, this was the wrong job for him. Jonathan thought the guy was about to hit him. It was not pretty. So after a quick, curt conversation that really could have been ugly, Jonathan handed his now ex-boss the key, said sorry one more time, and walked away.

MOVING ON FOR YOURSELF

For Kaplan, the decision to leave the political scene was not an easy one. He was faced with a dilemma that left him sleepless: He had several jobs that he knew would lead to a wonderful career, but he did not actually enjoy the jobs themselves and wasn't so sure that he was interested in the place the jobs were leading him. "I don't like how my experience here has changed me," he said at the time. "I am so cynical. Putting together someone's briefing book day in and day out is not what I imagined doing when I came to Washington, D.C."

Although some thought he was crazy for letting go of his job in the White House, he had a rare chance to compete in something he had dreamed of since childhood and a chance to get started on a sort of freelance writing tryout. So after some soul-searching, conversations with family and friends, and a visit to a local career counselor, he decided to bag the job and take on the Ironman.

He was certainly afraid of what the time off would do to his career possibilities, but his exit was a smart one. He tapped his resources and made sure he didn't burn any bridges with good and helpful contacts, he talked to a career counselor to help him line up his career strategies for before and after the triathlon, and he checked in with his contacts while he was training, telling them how he was doing and asking them to keep him abreast of any jobs that may fit his background and interests. One of those contacts worked for him. One day, he was in the gym talking to a guy who he had known for a year or two and who worked in White House personnel. He was familiar with Jonathan's plight and mentioned the Secretary of the Army was looking for a speechwriter. After a few interviews and review of

Jonathan's writing, he was offered the job, which would be waiting for him after the Ironman competition.

In the meantime, he got in touch with his other contacts: the print journalism kind. He began to pitch his story and got a piece into the *Washington Post* and another on National Public Radio. He did this so people could see that he had writing ability and so he would have a couple clips in his portfolio. But it wasn't entirely simple. He was turned down for a piece in the *New Republic*, which was devastating at the time. He also got a piece published about D.C. bachelor parties in Playboy.com (bet that was tough to research) and did some work for U.S. Representative Ken Bentsen. This time away from a 9-to-7 job at the White House helped him discover there was some opportunity to write out there. It was something he had always wanted to do, but it was too hard to jump off the career path he was on. "The Ironman gave me the excuse I needed," he said.

So after accomplishing his goal of competing in and completing the Ironman, Kaplan returned to Washington, D.C., in October of 2000, and started work with the Secretary of the Army. If it wasn't for his gumption to ask questions and take a chance, he pictured himself in one way: "I'd still be putting together briefing books, be 30 pounds overweight, and going through a bottle of St. John's Wort each week."

Those who hired him after the triathlon admired what he had done. They liked what he wrote while training, and they appreciated the fact that he took a chance. Because of the change of administration, he left a few months later, got married, and moved to New York, where he is a full-time freelance writer. "I never come home unhappy. I never come home at the end of the day and say, 'Why am I doing this?!'"

There are many people, like you, who come out of college and find they don't want to hop onto that subway to corporate America—maybe just for now, maybe forever. These years are your years to really learn about yourself, do some discovery, and enjoy the ride along the way. Take a chance; you never know what you can bump into. And say you choose to go to Alaska to tap sap. Fine. That's excellent. Just know that you're getting something out of it (other than syrup) and enjoy it. Even tapping sap will give you skills that are transferable to a future job and career.

Just because your parents expect you to take a job that the big guys offer doesn't mean you have to. You can pitch it to them in a way that might soothe their fears . . . mainly because the pitch is true. They need patience, just as you need patience.

8

What You're Learning

*M*att Edwards had no intention of sticking around, and he certainly didn't think his job offer to work at a large consulting firm was going to be a life-enhancing experience. He was a Spanish major; he liked to travel the world. He grew up in Zimbabwe before he moved to the United States as a young teen. Working for a big corporation was never something he expected himself to do, as I mentioned in the last chapter.

But he took a job as a computer programmer because he knew it was a paycheck to pay off student loans, and a good one at that.

Matt came out of college making $30,000. "I calculated it and was like "I get a $1,200 paycheck every two weeks!'" (And he thought: that's 240 subs at Subway! Woo hoo!). That was certainly amazing, after spending much of college paying for a beer with dimes. But that wasn't the best part of this job, he realized seven—yes, SEVEN—years later. What he really ended up with, he said, was a long lesson in how to deal with people, what drives people, and how to work with other people.

He realizes now that he just got paid to go through about seven years of a plush boot camp. He gained skills that he can carry with him forever, even if his work has nothing to do with computer programming, like it did at his consulting firm.

> It is the general skills you learn at your first jobs that really matter. Your specific job skill is of course very important, but it can be irrelevant in the face of a new career or job change. The computer program you worked on last year might be totally obsolete next year. But the folks who get ahead are the ones who master the broad skills learned in jobs along the way. You can apply them to anything.

Matt now spends his days in San Francisco thinking of a new plan. He was laid off last year in a wave of major layoffs. But he was practically on the verge of asking for a pink slip anyway. Once he learned his lessons in business and dealing with people, he realized he was ready to move on toward something that was more a part of who he is. But he wouldn't have been able to do much moving on at all without the first job that he expected would last only a year.

"I think your first job is providing the basics, kind of the fundamental skills that you couldn't have learned in college," he said. "They're not academic; like how to deal with people, how to motivate people, how to cooperate with people, how to forge alliances. That's something I really learned on my job." [Can anyone say "Survivor?"]?

Those are the skills that he will use in whatever he does with his life. He came into the job never suspecting he would gain those valuable things, he said. But he is realizing now that he can go back and apply those skills in a lot of different ways to many different projects. He can definitely apply it to his newest venture, moviemaking. "Because what is it? It's pulling together resources, creating a business case for why it should be done, and managing people, all who have very different skills. And empowering them to all do their thing so that the end product is successful," he said.

Basically, it's a different version of project management, which is what he ended up doing at the consulting firm. Who knew that a job at a big consulting company could help someone be successful at moviemaking? Well, I'm telling you: even if you don't love the job you are in right now, absorb those general skills. Absorb what you can absorb, and take those skills into the next thing that you do actually want to do.

Once you realize what you have learned, you will be able to transition into other jobs and appreciate the job you're in now. There were many times when I wondered why I was answering the phone for fellow reporters. I learned many things, including patience, how to deal with angry people and calm them down, and how to navigate communication professionally. Those skills I learned still help me today.

THIS IS *SO* NOT MY DREAM JOB

Here is someone else who picked up valuable skills from a job that she didn't necessarily have a major passion for. Sure, the jobs she has had to this point are fine, and they pay the bills, but they don't add up to her dream career. However, she knows that the things she has learned from these jobs will combine into a greater knowledge of the business world for when she decides to move toward her dream of starting her own business.

Ellie knew these were not her dream jobs, and working in sales for the rest of her life was not her goal. But the jobs she has had so far have provided her with skills, experience, and best of all, confidence. With that, she knows she will be able to accomplish her true love: to start her own business.

Ellie started life after college the way many of us do. She traveled a little and sent her résumé out haphazardly for administrative assistant openings. She didn't have a clue what she wanted to do. She had majored in sociology but says that is because it was the only major that could hold her interest for four years.

So when Ellie got an interview with a small printing company, she went to it, hoping to come out of the interview with a job as an admin. After an hour-and-a-half interview with the owner of the small company, he convinced her to skip a few steps and start out as an inside salesperson. She was afraid that she couldn't do it and sort of gave him a bunch of excuses. But he told her they would train her, and they did. "I'm really indebted to him," she says now.

Because the company was so small, she was able to get experience that people who have been in sales for years don't get. She had her own territory and had to hash out some difficult sales. She also became a manager rather quickly. "It really got my feet wet," she says. No matter what, she had a great résumé that showed her pretty incredible experiences. However, after a year and a half, she was ready to move on from this comfortable mom-and-pop.

As with many people her age, she figured it was time to check out the new dot-com phenomenon. So she hooked up with a friend, who helped her get a job at a San Francisco–based organization, where she did online advertising sales. The fantastic thing about that jump, she said, was that it tripled her salary immediately. Since she wasn't sure what she wanted to do in a macro way, the salary and experience she gained at her new gig would do for now. Figuring it all out later would come, well, later.

LEARNING IN *ANY* JOB

Even though she admits that doing sales for the rest of her life isn't her ultimate dream, she does acknowledge that this job has really provided her with invaluable skills that she can take with her to any job.

One thing that she found to be ultra-important, and something she wishes she could have convinced herself to do earlier than she did, is to not be afraid of titles. She was afraid of titles, and even though people told her to go straight to the top when calling companies to sell her product, she always started much lower in the food chain. She finally realized that she had only held herself back by not talking to the vice president— either at her own company or at the companies she called to sell her product. "I had been uncomfortable calling people at my same level. I was aiming so low. I had heard it over and over again: 'Talk to the decision maker.' Finally it just dawned on me that I should call the decision maker," she said. "The title didn't mean anything, and all of a sudden, it made so much less work for me."

She no longer had to call someone low on the title pole to sell a product, only to wait several weeks for that sales pitch to be passed along or to set up an appointment to talk with that person's boss. And no longer did she feel like "title-people" were invincible.

Because sales is so much about rejection and being able to handle rejection, she learned to grow confident, both with her calls and in the workplace itself.

She learned that it really helped to stake her own claim and set herself apart from the others. That thing that makes you stand out: focus on it. Doing something because it's easy and comfortable doesn't get you far, she said. "It makes you a follower rather than someone who is able to learn and get somewhere," she said.

At one of the dot-coms she went to after her first job, she suggested to an executive that she come to the higher-level meetings and take notes. The wrong information from the meetings, or no information at all, was being distributed to the salespeople. So she thought she could be the conduit. The boss did a "Huh, sure," and she was on her way. Sitting in on the meetings really helped her learn how dependent all the different units within a business are on each other. And she knew that if she wasn't there, the ad sales team wasn't going to get much information. As much as she didn't want to be looked upon as a secretary taking notes, she knew it was invaluable for her own knowledge.

So will she stick with a sales job? "I like this, I'll do this. But what it's taught me is I want to come up with my own business. I keep a binder of notes, where I write what businesses need and what they don't have. I think sales is a fantastic job to learn how to present yourself, networking. I know it's given me a great amount of skills. Being the underdog has really given me the competitiveness . . . the drive to get away from this."

She continued, "Seems so silly to me that my friends are so creative and [we] haven't put our heads together to do something. There's just so much creativity that we're not tapping into."

Maybe she and Matt should start something together. Hey, just a suggestion, man.

FIGURING IT OUT BY PROCESS OF ELIMINATION

No one ever told Elizabeth Matthews that she would go from being an idealistic college student with a major in anthropology and women's studies to a temp worker doing data entry for the National Restaurant Association. (During which time, all of her liberal friends thought she was working for the National Rifle Association. Get it?)

Nor did she know that her first temp job would be followed by another—this one with an extermination company whose files were set on fire by a competitor. Her job was to take the gasoline-soaked documents and reenter them into the database.

No. No one told her a degree would take her to these marvelous places. But it did. Key word, though, is temporary.

Elizabeth knew that the jobs were not permanent. They were there to pay the bills until she found a job she believed in, after she served as a Vista volunteer in Zimbabwe for the first year out of college. But one day, while trying to deal with the smell of the gasoline at the exterminator's office, she freaked. She started crying, left the office, and literally ran home and went to bed.

Sometimes, she said looking back, you just have to know when to split.

So split she did.

Entry-level jobs that often leave young workers frustrated are good for many reasons. One of the most important things they do is teach us what we *don't* want to do. This entry-level job can be the next step in your education, minus the loans. You get the class time in a culture and business environment you learn to like—or don't. And with that, you can start marking off the things you don't want, like filing gasoline-soaked records, and you can start listing the things that you do want. Take the time to think whether you like the casual dress the company abides by, or if you would rather be in a business suit. Do you like that the boss is the same age as your dad, or would you rather have someone who recently went through the same anxieties as you did?

After Elizabeth left her lovely (er, combustible) temp job, she started to talk to her friends and tried to focus her job search down to jobs with some meaning, maybe nonprofit work. She figured that without any big jobs on her résumé just yet, she would have to make her own contacts to gain entry into the working world. So she called her friends, family, and people she volunteered with to ask if they knew of openings at local nonprofits. Anything would do; she just wanted to get her foot in the door at a good organization. Then she could think about what came next.

Elizabeth soon heard from a friend about the Points of Light Foundation, something George Bush the elder put together to encourage volunteerism. Elizabeth balked a bit, being that she is a liberal Democrat, and at the time thought there wasn't anything a Republican president could do right. And to actually work for one? Well . . . .

So she let the organization's annual report—which her friend had handed to her—sit on her desk for a few weeks while she tried to find another job. And then she looked it over. Seemed like a decent organization, she thought, and it *is* a nonpartisan organization, after all. So she finally sent her résumé, went in for an interview, and then accepted a job offer.

She is so glad she took it. She learned a lot, got a decent salary, and got a feel for the nonprofit sector. (She's still voting for the Democrats, though.)

Sometimes, it pays to open your boundaries a little bit. Being a part of a national nonprofit, Elizabeth learned things, she experienced things, and she gained skills and made contacts. It wasn't necessarily the job of a lifetime, but it did give her a good boot-camp kind of start.

The good start is credited partly to the size of the organization. She was able, at age 23, to do things that she might not have been able to had she taken on a small job at a big organization. She began to ask coworkers and supervisors if she could just try to work in a few different departments so she could gain different skills and figure out what interested her. They went for it, and she was able to ask questions along the way. Her coworkers knew this was kind of a training ground for her, so they gave her freedom and answered her many questions. In the meantime, she made mental notes of what she liked and what she didn't like about the organization, and about the various departments and work she was trying out. The last department she worked for trained and consulted corporations that were building employee volunteer programs. Aha. That piqued her interest. "I got really intrigued with corporations trying to give back to the community," she says.

Like Elizabeth, anyone in his or her first real job should take note of what piques his or her interest, and what does just the opposite. Elizabeth did that and kept her eyes open for any other opportunities that gave her a rush just reading the job description.

If there is one thing Elizabeth would like to tell those who are just starting out, it is that you shouldn't worry if you don't graduate from college with a defined career path, like those who go on to law school or medical school. "Follow your gut instinct, and you'll be fine," she says. "Just because some of us don't fit into a traditional, defined career path, that doesn't mean you're not going to have a rewarding experience."

Finding what you don't like is just as important as figuring out what you do like. And it's often a little easier. I knew way back in grade school that I didn't want to do anything related to math. It went back to the timed addition tests Ms. Kelley gave us in first grade. But I won't go into the morbid details. Let's just say it wasn't pretty. That experience led me at an obviously early age to fear anything with numbers. I would always tell my mom that maybe I wanted to be an archaeologist. Or a zoo director. Or maybe a biologist. Each time I came up with a new career, though, I'd ask if it involved math. If it did, that was it for that career path. Hence, I majored in English. I guessed reading and writing were as far away from math as anything could be.

That stuck with me throughout college and into my first jobs after college. Granted, I do have to use math sometimes now as a business reporter, but I just count on my fingers when I need to. (Kidding, really.)

More than the bigger picture of finding out what kind of job you don't want, this is a good time to figure out what kind of culture and atmosphere you don't want. Rachel Brown, for instance, quickly learned at 22 that her life outside of work is still very important to her. "I realized my lifestyle is much more important than I thought," says the employee at a large consultancy. "I thought I could work long hours, but I can't. I can't have a job that consumes me 24/7." So emulating friends who work as investment bankers or at large law firms is out of the picture. Her next job she interviews for, she'll be sure to find a place where life and work can be separate. That's what is important to her.

SHOULD I HIT THE ROAD?

It's easy to come out of school and take the first job offer that comes your way. But it can also be dangerous. Because if it's not what you would really like to do with your life, you may let yourself get stagnant and stick it out a little too long. Not good. You should give yourself some goals, and if you don't reach them, think about moving on.

If you aren't handed that pink slip, sometimes it's just too hard to quit a job that doesn't thrill you but does protect you and provide you with a steady paycheck and some sort of benefits package.

Sue Schulz said she was always very humble about her job as a gossip column clipper for the magazine. But eventually, she said, "I was, like, I went to college to read gossip columns and cut them up? I was kinda like, 'What's the point of this?'"

When you hit that crossroad, it may be time to move on.

Sometimes the hardest decision anytime in our career, but especially when we're young, is figuring out when it's time to hit the road, vamoose, take our boots and start walking. On the one hand, you can assume that your next job will be a step up with better pay and benefits. On the other, you can assume that if you stick it out where you are, the harder you work, the more you'll move up. Problem is, you're probably right on both counts. So how do you decide what's next?

FINDING THE PERFECT (OR PERFECT FOR NOW) FIT

Oh, it used to seem so simple. Take the job you're offered, go to work. At the office. Go home at 5. Come back at 9. Repeat.

Thank goodness it's not so simple anymore. The newest generation of workers really has a ton of choices, even with an economic slowdown. You can make up your own path, much more easily than generations before you. With the onslaught of the Internet, of many new start-ups, and attitudes about work that have changed over the years, you have choices.

Before you look into a job seriously, or a move out of the one you're in, there are many things you should look at with the organization. What is the culture like? What do employees wear? How old or young are most of the employees? What's the pecking order? How quickly do people leave? Is it a big company or small organization? What's the growth potential?

These questions can be answered in many ways, but especially when you pose them. In other words, *ask*. Interviews are not just a place to show the employer that you're the one they want; it's a time for you to ask these questions and interview the person interviewing you. It's natural to feel that the interview is a test of you as a prospective employee. But that's not the way it should be. This is the time to ask right back, and to put the employer in the hot seat—kindly, of course.

The most important thing to remember is that a job interview should not be about you and how you answer questions, but it should be about a mutual fit.

Dan Sondhelm remembers how he made his decision about the office culture. He was offered jobs from larger financial firms, and he was offered a job where he was interning. It was a small start-up, where as an intern, he had duties like Fed

Exing and faxing, along with sitting in on client meetings and going to financial conferences. At a larger firm, he realized, yes, he may get paid more, but he'd have fewer chances to get the hands-on experience he would at the start-up. He knew that he would have many older mentors to help him at the larger firm, but he could get lost in the large number of employees at the firm. At the start-up, he had a chance to grow with the company, and he had the ability to talk to the president constantly: There were only a handful of people at the company when he signed on. He knew that a smaller firm, where he could try new things without going through many levels of bosses, would be the best fit for him.

Obviously, an annual report and some corporate Web sites will give you information about the company with which you're interviewing. But there are other ways to really get a feel for a job and an organization.

Don't be afraid to ask your interviewer if you can talk to potential coworkers. Interviewers are fine, but remember, they are trying to sell something. The more questions you ask to many different people, the more you'll know about what you're getting yourself into.

Ask people what a typical day is like, how much interaction they have with their supervisors, and what kind of feedback they get. General mood of the workplace, how long it took them to move onto fun projects, and how open the open-door policy really is are all things to ask about.

WHEN TO BAIL

The signs may not be too obvious (or maybe just not as obvious as they were for Elizabeth), so this issue as to whether to move on or not, as with anything, will take a lot of self-reflection. This is the point where people wish they would get laid off. That way, they wouldn't have to reflect and decide if they should move on. That would be decided for them. Oh joy.

Some signs that it may be time to get going: Collecting a paycheck just doesn't do it for you anymore. The boss gives you the same work week after week, and despite your attempts at gaining new experiences and projects, it just ain't happening. And sometimes, you sit back and realize that your boss, supervisors, and coworkers continue to look at you as the new kid on the block and have no plans to look at you in any other light. Sometimes those higher-ups see you as a junior employee and have no intention of changing that outlook. If you've tried to change their point of view about you and it doesn't seem to work, then it's probably time to hit the job search trail again.

Sometimes it helps to write down the pros and cons of your job situation. You may not realize just how many things you've already realized about your job but haven't yet translated into action at work. You learn these things so gradually sometimes that you learn them and then don't do anything about them. But these things that you have learned—if you sit down and think about what they are—can be translated into new and better skills for a new and better job. You just hadn't taken the time to think about it yet. A list might draw that out much more clearly for you.

There comes a time when you really have to kick yourself out of that comfort zone and take a chance on that next big thing.

When you're not having fun anymore and you don't think you can move up, then go seek out something you're going to grow from, in, with. Let it be something that you want to do when you wake up in the morning, and not something you start to dread when Sunday afternoon rolls around.

Some people know with amazing clarity the moment they absolutely, no doubt have to move on. Like Paolo Audiberti. He went to Georgetown University to study English and was also big into computers. While he was there, he began to intern at a local dot-com and did their Web design, then wrote code for them. When he graduated, they offered him a job. He took it and did fine. He played with computers, worked long hours, got paid well. And then?

"One day I freaked out. I was walking home from the supermarket and was like, 'Is this it?' I have a comfy job, I'm making money, and then I'll get married, have kids, die. I need to get the hell out of here. So I rolled out," he said. He can't explain it beyond that. It just hit him one day in his early twenties that if he stayed in Washington, D.C., much longer, he wasn't going to take a chance at anything else, and he'd just stick around in his comfortable life. "Something inside me was like, 'You need to go, man.'" And so he went.

After growing up in New York City, he knew he'd like to return. He also knew that he wanted more computer knowledge. So he applied to New York University for a master's in computer science, and was accepted. He moved back to the city, started school and began to help friends who needed computer work, coding, Web design. And he and some friends even started their own company. He hopes to someday do computer-generated special effects for movies.

Don't be afraid to move on, if you think that's what's right for you right now. When you are hired, your boss should look at you as someone that he *wants* to move up and out of an entry-level job. If he doesn't ask for that or mention that when you ask about what kind of career development or growth they have at the organization, the red flags should go up. Any good boss will want you to move up, even if that means he will lose an entry-level worker every few months. Your desire to do more than what's expected of you will help you gain entry into jobs that you want.

TAKING A CHANCE THAT TURNS OUT TO BE . . . WRONG

Sue Schulz, *CosmoGirl* editor, didn't get there as easily as it may seem. In fact, she made a choice or two along the way that just seemed all wrong to her once she found herself in the situation. But now, of course, she sees the perks of those bad decisions and realizes that she made the best of them. But what happens when you find yourself in that situation?

Before she became an editor at *CosmoGirl*, Sue worked for *YM*. She worked there while the dot-com excitement was going on around her, and she started to feel like she was missing out . . . missing out on being a part of a new company, missing out on the excitement of a dot-com full of young people, and certainly missing out on the potential stock options that were headed the way of many twenty-somethings at the time.

So after thinking about it for a while, she accepted a job that was offered to her at a dot-com in New York City. She was excited to move on and was ready for a new challenge. Her friends and cohorts at *YM* all asked if she was sure she wanted to make such a drastic change, but she really felt she was. A few days before her first day at the dot-com, she went out and treated herself to a new outfit and some spa treatments. Then the day before her big day, the dot-com's founder called her. Um, hey there, Sue, um, no reason for you to come in tomorrow. Our money from a potential venture capitalist never came through.

Ugh. She had quit her job and been replaced already. And not only that, she was afraid to tell everyone what happened, mostly because of the ego factor. She knew her former coworkers wouldn't make fun of her, but she really felt like she crashed and burned. Hard. And fast.

A couple days after regrouping, she gathered herself together and began calling her former coworkers at various magazines. No one really had a job opening at the time, but they did have some projects that needed to be taken care of. So Sue took on her newest venture: freelancing.

Making a bad decision doesn't always mean it's a bad decision. For Sue, that decision to leave *YM* led to her job as an editor at *CosmoGirl*, which at the time was a new, exciting adventure, much like the many dot-coms that were booming.

But say you chose a job that you thought was right for you, good for your career, and potentially fun. But then you find out you were way wrong. For Sue, the signs were simple . . . the job (and the company) just didn't exist anymore. She didn't have to tell her new boss that she made a bad choice. He took care of that for her.

Bailing quickly on a job is a scary and complicated situation and decision. You may doubt your gut feeling, and you may think you have to listen to your parents who tell you that you must stay in a job for at least a year before you move on. Take that as good advice you can tuck away, but not necessarily advice you have to act on immediately.

Like Jonathan Kaplan's decision, it is possible to right a wrong. It will probably be torturous, but only for a little while.

In most circumstances, most people would automatically assume that you do something like this, and you ruin your career. But that's certainly not so, and certainly was not the case for Jonathan. Yes, his was probably not the best situation to be in, but the fact is, we make mistakes. Sometimes we make a big wrong decision. It's all part of discovering what we want out of life and out of a career. The important thing to remember is you are never truly stuck in a situation you don't want to be in. There is a way out, and even if that way out is not so graceful (like our friend Jonathan), it is necessary and you'll be so glad you did it later. Nothing is permanent in this career world if you don't want it to be. If you make a wrong decision, you fix it. It's just important to figure out if you really made a bad decision or you need to work on your situation where you are. And if you decide that you made the wrong decision, sit down and figure out how you did it and why and how you won't do it again. And as much as possible, fix that wrong decision with grace. But no matter what, do it.

When you figure out what is wrong with the job, decide if it's something you can talk to your new supervisor about. Many people say they took a job believing it was one thing, only to find out later they had much different duties than they were told in the interview. That's the perfect time to express your concern to that person who hired you. Tell that person what your expectations were, and what you see the reality is. Then express why that doesn't work well for you. Then check out the response. If it doesn't meet your satisfaction, it may be time to pull that résumé out again and think of a new way to look at this potentially ugly situation.

One 28-year-old found herself in that situation recently. She took a job in technology support and found out rather quickly that it wasn't what she thought it was going to be. "There were things that just weren't told to me. The position I was going for, I took a step back. I expressed my issues in the beginning, and they said they would take care of it. It didn't happen." When she realized almost immediately that she was overqualified for the job she ended up in, she went to the recruiter, team leaders, and then a human resource manager. The human resource manager said the organization would work on placing her in another position, but that didn't pan out. She knew it was time to go . . . just a few weeks into the job.

SO WHY HIRE ME AFTER THAT?

So here's the big question. Once you've decided that you made the wrong choice and it's time to leave, how do you sell yourself to that next potential employer? "Um, hi. I'd like to tell you I was on an intellectual romp throughout Asia these last two months, but in fact, I was falling through the nine layers of hell. So hire me."

Explaining why you split so soon after taking a job can be tricky. A potential boss might think you were forced to leave, and truth is, a lot of employers whose employees leave after a record short period of time might not be too keen on you. Don't expect them to stick up for you when a hiring manager calls to ask why you're not there anymore. With that in mind, try to make the departure as amicable as possible. That way, you may not get a sterling recommendation, but you also might be saved from some bad press.

From there, figure out exactly what it is you're willing to disclose in an interview. Be sure you have something in mind before you're in the hot seat, because you will be asked what you've been doing these last few weeks or months. This is a time when truthfulness, to some extent, is a good thing. (Okay, that's just about always, but especially now.) You can tell your employer that you made a mistake. If you can come up with a couple of solid reasons why that was a mistake, good. Don't be too vague, and definitely don't tell too much. Explain that now that you've made that mistake, you have a much better feel for what you and a company should be for each other. It was a learning experience (right?), and you learned from that experience just what you want in a job from here on out. If you want to tell them more about the experience, or if they ask, go ahead. Just don't drag your former employer through the mud, and don't act bitter. Your potential employer will see that as the potential you, and she might think you will do that to her as well.

As for Sue, when her former coworkers found out about her bad choice, they didn't hold it against her. She went on to free-lance for a bit and was later offered the interview with *Cosmo-Girl*. She laughs about her experience in the dot-com world now and knows that it was for the best. She got her taste of free-lancing that she might never have had.

To avoid the sticky situation again of a job that just isn't what you wanted, be more careful the next time around. Go ahead and ask your new potential employers to put their offer in writing. There is nothing wrong with asking an employer-to-be to write a formal letter with the details of your new job, such as title, duties, and start date. That will ensure you have something in writing if you find yourself running your boss's errands instead of working on ad campaigns, which you were hired for. It will also assure you that you're going into a job you actually desire.

Don't be afraid that you're asking too many questions in an interview. This is your time to check *them* out and make sure the job and offer is good for both of you. The 28-year-old who found herself in the wrong job says the same thing. "Ask what you'll be doing day to day. Go as far as to say you'd like to meet the people you'll be working with," she said. "I thought I was going to move forward in my career, but this was really a step back."

Just remember that we all make mistakes, and sometimes we just have to accept them as experience, and move on to the next thing. Beats the hell out of crying all the time.

WHEN THE GOING GETS BAD . . .

Lilly, the telecom maven we mentioned earlier, is from Mexico, and she went to school in Florida for both high school and college. Because of her background, and partly because she was a woman in a very male-dominated field of telecommunications, it seems that one of her bosses felt she was an easy target to push around.

"My boss was really condescending at times, especially because of the nationality issue," she said. "He would say things like 'In the U.S., we do it like this.' Meanwhile, I've been living here for 15 years!"

She felt her boss was constantly waiting for her to make typos or grammatical errors in emails or other documents. "It was really hard, because I became extra paranoid about it. By the end, that hurt my productivity." It was very frustrating for Lilly, who didn't feel like she had any control over the situation. It was her second job, this one at a start-up, and the job market was pretty challenging, yet she couldn't wait to leave. Lilly was on a temporary visa while she worked there, and the company she was at was supposed to apply for her H1B visa, which would last for a long time. "If I were to quit or be fired, then I'd be pretty lost. So I always felt like he had the upper hand," she said. Because of that, she let him have his way and tried to make his remarks and attitude slide off her shoulders.

But toward the end, she was sick of the demeaning comments and horrible work environment. She couldn't wait to quit, despite the rough job market at the time and her visa situation. The first opportunity she had to leave, she took it.

It's tough when you have a situation that really may not be fixable in any means normally available. And there just comes a time when you have to decide what you can put up with, what you can fix, and what is a sign that it's just time to move on.

MAKING A GRACEFUL EXIT

How you depart from a job might be just as important as how you search and interview for a new job. Remember that you never know what life might bring and what your own psyche may do to you years down the road. You may want to come back. Or more likely, you may want to work somewhere with the people you left a few years back for that more exciting job.

Sue Schulz has had a bunch of experience with this situation, having left a handful of jobs to go on to other opportunities, all before the age of 30. When she left a job as a senior editor at *YM magazine* to run off to a dot-com, she made sure to smooth the transition as much as possible, in case she ever wanted to come back to the magazine world. Good thing she did, because the dot-com went dot-bomb the day she started her new job.

But when she decided to leave *YM*, she felt that it was okay to do so. She had put in a solid year as a senior editor and two years as an associate editor. "I feel that if you give somebody a year of your service, they cannot get mad at you for moving on." Because she worked really hard, and because she stayed at *YM* for a solid amount of time, she felt that her coworkers and fellow editors were happy that she was happy with her new decision to leave.

"Most times, people will be glad that you have the guts to do it. If they hear you were offered something and didn't take it, they will wonder why you didn't take it," she says. Not that it matters what other people think, but it does help lighten the load a bit to remember that you are not an indentured servant to Company X.

Sue said it is important when you leave a job not to leave any loose ends. Before she left *YM*, she worked late hours and came in on a Saturday to make sure that not only her work was done but also that the person moving into her position would be prepared. "Don't leave skid marks on the way out," she advised. Let your coworkers, and the person taking your job, know where to reach you, because during those first weeks that you are gone, "you fortify that bridge," Sue said. You not only want to be a loyal employee, you also want to be a loyal ex-employee. "Don't ever burn a bridge, even if you are like, 'Good riddance.' Because you know what? You'll end up working with that person you screwed over in a year."

Sue is glad she smoothed things over before she left, because once she found out the dot-com would cease to exist, she immediately called her friends and coworkers at *YM* to ask if they knew of any freelance projects she might be able to work on while she figured things out.

FINDING CONNECTIONS

I know I've told you that it's good to meet people because they will be the reason you move on, and they might be able to help you find a job when you decide it's time to get into something new. But as a brand-new worker, you probably wonder where the heck you're going to find all these people.

Surely, you can't ask the guy in Office B if he has any connections to the real estate industry. But maybe that person next to you will be a contact soon. As Sue Schulz said, don't worry now if you don't have a connection somewhere, or contacts all over the place. You will. Your five best friends from your first company will go on to different organizations. They will meet new people who will be looking for someone to help with a new business, or at a company they are moving to, and your friend will remember the perfect person for that job. You.

The reason Sue first was considered for *CosmoGirl* was because a friend she worked with at *YM* moved to the magazine earlier. But this person didn't just move from *YM* to *CosmoGirl* by answering an ad in the newspaper (not that there's anything wrong with that). She knew the editor-in-chief at *CosmoGirl*, which was a brand-new magazine at that time, because the editor-in-chief used to be an intern for the woman at an organization before *YM*! Breathe, breathe. Okay.

Then when the editor-in-chief told her new employee (who used to manage her when she was an intern) that they needed a deputy editor, Sue's friend from *YM* immediately thought of Sue. She interviewed, and she got the job several weeks later.

DON'T BURN BRIDGES . . . EVEN IF

So, all the advice I have given to you (with the help of those who were willing to share their stories) about the contacts you'll make without even trying, and how your friends may end up being the connection to a great job in the future, you may have been able to figure out on your own. But it never hurts to have some reminding. I know many people can forget this one sometimes, especially after a heated argument or two.

Obviously, stuff happens at work where you find yourself in a situation of, well, not really liking someone. Or you get yourself into a little disagreement. But you really should not even let a conflict at work last. First of all, it's not doing anyone any good (man, can't we all just get along?). But suppose that person who you like least and whose chair you kept stealing turns out to be the one with the connection to a job you want the most. Don't let it get to that. Always make an effort to smooth things over, not just so you can use them later (is that what this sounds like?), but so you can live peacefully at work, and then so you can use them later. (I joke. Kind of.)

Holding a grudge in today's workplace is going to be a tough thing for you to handle down the road. I see many people and hear many stories of people who end up working with someone they used to tease, talk about, ignore, or otherwise just be not nice to. And that person ends up as a supervisor. Or that person knows the supervisor. Or the person who holds the grudge finds his dream job, then finds that his one contact related to the organization is that old guy he used to disagree with constantly, to the point where he couldn't even talk to him anymore.

"Everyone hires their friends," says Sue. "So many times when you need a person quickly, a person to fill that great position, you think of people you know. It becomes sort of incestuous. So you can never burn a bridge." Amen, sister.

GETTING CANNED

When I graduated from college, I walked right into what soon became the biggest economic boom this country has ever seen. My friends and people I wrote about were constantly battling what job offer, out of several, to take. They wondered if they should take the one with millions of dollars of possible stock options or the one with the chance to head up the entire Web development department at the dot-com.

Then things changed. In the last few years, dot-coms have gone bust. Layoffs are just part of everyday situations. And companies are not scrambling to expand and fill cubicles like they once were.

But that doesn't mean that a job search is impossible. In fact, it doesn't mean that getting laid off is the world's worst situation. It can mean opportunity.

Getting laid off isn't all bad. Sure, there are those months of no work, but then there are, well, those months of no work. It's a perfect time to rethink your life. It's the perfect "out" from a job that just didn't fit. And if it did fit? Well, it's the perfect time to take those newly acquired skills and contacts and move into something you *know* now that you are into.

There's a bright side to getting canned. But it's so important to take the time to do some self-analysis and really move toward your next awesome step. It's the perfect opportunity to talk to former employers about what they think of your work, what they saw as great potential, and what they thought you needed to improve. You can take this time to shadow someone whose job sounds interesting or to volunteer at several different organizations to get a feel for what you might like to do or what kind of organization you might like to be a part of.

Take Matt Edwards. After seven years with the same company, he was laid off in 2001. Months before his pink slip, he told me that getting laid off might not be such a bad thing. He's a very creative person with many different thoughts and philosophies about life and what that whole life and work world should be like. But he had this great job . . . one that he actually tried to quit more than once, but each time he did, they offered him more money, or a promotion. Like the time he tried to quit so he could travel in Africa. His boss offered him the time off even though he didn't have vacation time built up. But then the tide turned. The company had lost a lot of money, and his job as a computer programmer was not in demand as much as it was when companies needed the software he helped to create and sell. After Matt had to lay off some people on his team himself, he got his own "letter of separation." (Otherwise known as: he was canned.) His company actually offered him another job, but he would have to leave his great life in San Francisco, something he didn't want to give up just yet.

So he remains, a few months later, officially unemployed. However, he is taking this time to check out other opportunities. He and his friend are in the process of creating a sort of rent-as-you-go movie studio space. They bought the equipment and rent the space, and local artists and wanna-be moviemakers pay them to use the cameras and studio space.

He also uses this time to read and even think about when he might leave San Francisco. He thinks Charlottesville, Virginia, or Boulder, Colorado, might hold his interest for a bit. So when his severance runs out—he will move on. But he'll do so intelligently and will know where to go from here.

Companies have to downsize. It's going to happen in just about everyone's lifetime at some point—or maybe you won't get laid off ever. But you will likely hear of others who are told their time is up.

So, you clean out your desk, take your boxes home to your efficiency apartment. Then what?

First of all, come up with a strategy. When Elizabeth Matthews was laid off from a technology company in Northern Virginia, she immediately emailed all of her friends, family, and former coworkers. She checked emails in the morning and tried to schedule lunch with someone every day. And in between? She made sure to get out of her apartment. A bike ride, a stroll through a museum, a walk to the zoo . . . whatever it took to get inspired, she did it. Then she came home in the afternoon and checked in with her contacts, emailed them, and read up on the most recent want ads.

Your strategy should include what you think the ideal job looks like. Take some time to sit down and write a list. Think about what kind of culture you like, what management style fits you, and what growth possibilities you might want. Then go out and network. Give people your pitch that you have come up with: You want, say, a relaxed culture, but one that has a career development program in place for its younger workers. A mentor system that is already set up would be great, and maybe you really like someone whose management style is not micro, but more macro. Someone who lets you run with your ideas but is more than willing to rein you in and give you feedback.

This is another very important time to not be shy. One twenty-something we'll call Sara Jones was laid off from a small communications firm in D.C. She immediately let her former clients, colleagues, friends, and family know about her sudden layoff. The response for leads for new jobs was encouraging. A week or two after her pink slip, she visited Philadelphia and New York, where she saw friends, had a drink with contacts, lunch with other contacts, dinner with, well, other contacts.

"It's like confetti. Personal friends of mine have told other people" and so on, she says. Her advice to others in the same situation? Get started immediately. "It's really important right after it happens, whether you're shocked or not, to get motivated in that first week. Make a list of what you have to do," she suggests. "That way, if you're sitting in your apartment or in a coffee shop, you don't feel like there's a bottomless pit."

This is also the time to really search out and attend networking events and job fairs. Use every avenue there is to get to a place you want to be. Jeff Morris, 28, was laid off from a job with an aerospace publication in early 2001. He figured the more he got the news—and himself—out there, the more chances he would have at finding a new and better job.

He posted his résumé online and made himself attend a networking fair run by a group that holds monthly events in various cities nationwide. He likens networking to an awkward high school dance, but knows that just getting out there helps. Even if going is to lament his lost job with others . . . misery loves company. And sometimes misery has a contact or heard of a job offer he or she would like to share.

> It is a good time, when you're laid off, to try to get more than one job offer. That way, you have a choice. If you work to just get one offer, there won't be a choice, and you will have to jump at the first thing you get, even if the job isn't a great fit or doesn't thrill you.

Make sure the next job you take will advance your career. The key to any job search is to not jump too quickly into another wrong thing. The worst thing to do after receiving a goodbye note is to brood. You have got to get out of the apartment, stop your whining, and start doing things, even if they do not necessarily mean a job offer.

This is the time to think about your accomplishments—not just for your interviews; it will also make you feel better and help you to figure out where you excel. Not only do you need to list accomplishments, you need to think about why these are important and how you accomplished them. Think about what you did, how you did it, and what was the end result. And think in tangible examples. What about that problem you encountered? What happened? What did you do to try to remedy the situation, and then what happened when you did that?

HEADHUNTERS

Another job search tool to check out is the headhunter. Don't like that name? How about recruiter? Job finder and seeker. Sorta counselor, good advice giver.

The headhunter can be a great tool in your job search, both early on and if you are let go from an organization. One thing to remember, however, is that a headhunter is not there to simply match you up with your dream job. You can't just kick back and tell Recruiter X to find you a job and call you when it's all over. You have to do some work too.

And another important thing to remember: Don't take the job just because he or she found it for you. It's a tough, yet common, situation to navigate. I remember talking to my roommate a couple years ago when her headhunter found her a job at a company that just didn't thrill her. The headhunter got impatient when my roommate said she wasn't sure that was the kind of company or atmosphere she wanted to be a part of. But the recruiter kept selling the spot, saying that there was advancement, a good salary, and benefits . . . all things my roomie didn't have at the time. But my roommate also knew she didn't want to take the job. So she struggled and looked for advice, but thankfully stuck to her decision.

The thing about recruiters is they get paid by a company to find an employee. So they *want* to get you a job. That's both good and bad. The good side is this can really be a great relationship that works out for you. But the bad side is, you may get a little push to take a job that really isn't for you. So be aware, but don't fret too much. More often than not, the recruiter you work with will understand your needs, skills, and desires and will do his or her best to put you somewhere that makes you happy. It's important for a recruiter to do that. After all, you're the one giving the recommendations to your friends, after your recruiter places you at that awesome company.

There are different kinds of recruiters. Some are generalists who place people in various jobs. Others are specific to an industry, such as a financial services recruiter. And then there is the executive recruiter, for management types who typically make $70,000 or more. We're really not going to talk about those guys here.

Jud Allen is a recruiter with Spectrum Financial Services in McLean, Virginia. He recruits for finance and accounting positions. And being in his late twenties himself, he knows what young job seekers are experiencing.

One thing he wants them to know, however, is that a recruiter is not necessarily there to help you find a new and different kind of job or experience from what you've already had. Companies want recruiters to find them employees with experience, no matter how small, and especially experience in a particular field.

In other words, Jud is not going to take an artist with no background in numbers to work at an accounting firm (unless the job is to be the in-house art director). It would not benefit him, and it would not benefit his client, the company.

But he will be fine passing you along to someone who may be able to place you in an art-related job.

There are several steps to getting someone like Jud to work with you. First is a phone conversation. He uses that time to assess how well a potential candidate speaks, what the person's background is, and what sort of work he or she wants—not necessarily in that order. Then the job seeker sends Jud a résumé. He decides whether the worker's skills are something that might match his clients' needs. Next is a sit-down interview with Jud, where he and the job seeker discuss, in more detail, goals, desires, and background.

It's important for job seekers to do some of the legwork for recruiters as well. The more you interact with a recruiter, the more leads the recruiter will be able to flip your way. Tell the recruiter if you hear of an interesting opening somewhere: he or she might know someone at the organization. And if not, the recruiter can still call the organization up and tell them that a great candidate is sitting, ready for a job.

Another good point to remember is that it's fine to go to more than one recruiter at a time. Find a specialized recruiter, if you have a specific career track, and find a general recruiter as well. Those recruiters are good at finding work for you near your house, or near a place you want to be. Choosing one recruiter from each type is a sort of "cover-your-bases" move.

So as you deal with the shock of a pink slip, remember that finding a new job is possible. Sadly (or not), there were many, many people who went before you and survived just fine.

9

This Is Preparation Time For . . . ?

*B*rian Mendelson's[1] career path thus far has led him through rather traditional, corporate routes. But it has been each step and each change that has led him to a point now where he feels he can fulfill whatever his dream may be, thanks to the skills, knowledge, contacts, and scars he has received throughout his first years out of college. Each jump has been a pretty huge one.

When Brian first graduated from the University of Virginia with a degree in business, with a focus in information systems, he went the traditional big-box company route. He signed on at Andersen Consulting. It was, he said, a crazy place to work. Many of his workweeks totaled 80 or 90 hours of office time. But it was also a great training ground. He was new to the workforce, he wanted to do information technology work, but he didn't want to get caught in a telecom firm, where he also had job offers, because he felt that young workers get lost in the mix and would not get real work to delve into. He

---

[1] His name has been changed.

felt that was not the case with Andersen. He knew the company had a special setup for new workers, where diving in headfirst was sort of the name of the game.

So dive he did, almost into burnout. After a year or so, Brian started to think that he'd had enough. After a while, he felt his skills weren't being puffed up, and like most younger workers at the company, after the initial learning curve, he was handed very structured work to do. That's good for some people, but Brian wanted more freedom and an ability to expand his skills and interests. These conclusions just happened to coincide with the burgeoning Internet industry. So as many in the mid-to-late 1990s did, Brian found an Internet start-up and hopped on board. Call that the Major Jump #1.

Being that the start-up was a much, much smaller organization, Brian had much, much more responsibility, which was both good and bad. Because the company had only a couple clients, Brian had to do what he could to hang on to them. If a client he was working with at Andersen disappeared, no big deal. There were thousands of others. Here, if a client left, the start-up might fold.

Brian had a hand in just about everything at the start-up. Being that he was only the fifth employee to be hired at the company, he helped with everything from designing the software to actually naming the organization (which has since been sold and folded into a much larger company).

But he soon realized the problem at the start-up was there was actually too much responsibility at a young age. Yes, he was gaining some incredible experience, but he also felt that perhaps he needed more training before taking on the aspect of this job that he had been handed. There was a lot of pressure, and he worked about 100 hours a week. Again, Brian realized the things he learned here were great, but not really what he wanted out of life. "I was still pretty young, so I was making career decisions focusing on career progression rather than personal progression," he says. Prepare for Major Jump #2.

He realized that everything he did took him a few steps farther in the career world and gave him additional skills, but as he was flying along, he barely had time to stop and think if this progression was actually the kind of progression he *wanted.* There are so many people in this world, and unfortunately, an inordinate number of people especially in our parents' generation, who didn't, or felt they couldn't, take the time to figure out if this career they were sailing along in was actually a career they wanted and loved. Brian realized young enough—which you can do too— that *he* could really be the one to decide what he wanted out of a career. There are so many options and so many different things to be done in this world, he knows there is something out there today that he can take on with his skills he gained, and something that fits with his interests. In the meantime, he knows that earlier jobs he had, where he learned and experienced many things, will be the path that leads him to be able to do what he truly wants to do.

When Brian first realized that he could do more than what he was doing, and do something he actually loved, he revamped his life a bit. In his mid-twenties at this point, he realized that he didn't necessarily want to be the technologist, he didn't necessarily want to make the product. But he did want to lead the people who do. "I don't know if it was immediate, if a lightbulb went off. But you start thinking about your skill set. You examine what you're good at and what you enjoy. I was an okay technologist and developer, but I hated it," he says. "What I enjoyed in the past was leading people and managing people around those projects. I don't like nitpicking over variables in designing development software. But I'm glad I had that experience, because I can lead people in the future who do this." And he knew he couldn't really do that without an MBA, so he began to apply to schools. Big Jump #3.

So Brian took some time off before school to think and took a little walk (ha) for about six months on the Appalachian Trail—the entire way from Georgia to Maine. It was the perfect time to spend thinking about life and what he wanted to do with his skills and time. Reflecting on his life to that point, 30-year-old Brian now realizes that he goes through cycles, and he thinks many of his friends and colleagues his age have done the same. The cycle he sees is preparation, achievement, and reflection. Up to this point, Brian had prepared by going to school. Then he achieved for almost five years at Andersen and the start-up. Then he took time on the trail to reflect and figure out what it was that those steps to that point had done for him, and what he wanted to do with that material he had gained and the MBA he would receive. And then he again began to prepare at school.

After graduation from graduate school, Brian knew that at 27, he would have to have a little luck shine his way if he expected to get a management position so young. And that's what happened. A manager at Hewlett-Packard took a chance on him. Brian had met him before, and the man thought Brian had a good, appropriate background, but also knew someone had to give him an in if he ever would get to manage. HP was the company to do that. "I was selling myself, and I guess they had a good feeling and gave me a chance," Brian said.

He took the job, and admits that it has been very tough. Despite the fact his hours are less than at former jobs, being a manager takes a ton of mental energy that exhausts him much more than long hours spent doing what he is told by a manager. "I'm zapped. You have 10 people looking at you, asking you what they should do. You know the goal, but you have to figure out how to get there," he said. When he first got to the job, he was totally overwhelmed. But he adjusted with time. "You make a few mistakes, learn from them, and move on. Time moves on and you learn things and realize you make fewer mistakes."

Brian again realizes that he's at a point where he can really buy into the whole preparation, achievement, and reflection cycle. But he feels that with those stages, there is a bigger cycle of those stages going on, and these first almost-10 years out of school are still a preparation time.

"I've had school, and a couple successes. And I think what I've been doing is finding out what I'm good at. I'm discovering what Brian can do, what my basic skill set is. But what I don't have is ultimate purpose," he says. "But I don't feel I'm wasting my time right now. I'm getting better and better at what I'm best at. But what I haven't found is what I'm going to work for. When I do go to work, I want to do a good job. At the end of each day, I feel good about it." But also at the end of each day, he knows that his skills are being spent on something that isn't necessarily what he wants to spend his skills on. Does it matter to him—the personal Brian—if HP makes another cent on its stock price? Probably not. But he knows that HP is a "vessel through which I can continue preparing until it's time for achievement and reflection."

Brian realizes that everything to this point has been planned; there have been lessons and guidelines: How to get out of school, how to get a job. But then there suddenly aren't guidelines, and you're the one who can write them, if you decide to take that chance. I hope this book has provided you with some stories and guidance to also make you feel that way. What you're doing right now is actually finding a direction for your own life.

"What I worry about and don't want to happen to me is I get to age 55 and I'm still working at a corporation and still reflecting. And I don't want to get to that point and be pissed that I didn't find my purpose," he says. So his advice to himself, his friends, and anyone who will listen? "Make sure you remember to get out of the preparation stage at some point." It seems that Brian is well on his way.

NOT THE END

And so goes the first stage of your lifelong pursuit of finding that awesome career that fulfills your dreams, goals, and desires. Alright, so maybe it sounds a lot easier than it is. But that's okay. It will be hard trying to figure out what step you should take along the way. Just remember that this is the perfect time to try things, reflect a lot, and focus on you. You only have one life, and a fitting, interesting, and lush career goes hand-in-hand with a fulfilling life.

These years just out of school are the time to analyze yourself, your talents and abilities, and how you can fit in to the greater world picture. First jobs are sort of a boot camp, where you gain skills that you can apply to that life and career you decide that you want for yourself. Or as Brian Mendelson says, this time now is preparation time for whatever it is you decide to do.

Good luck, and while you're at it, make sure to have fun.

Index

About The Author

AMY JOYCE currently writes the weekly "Life at Work" column for the *Washington Post*. She also hosts the "Live at Work" live discussion at WashingtonPost.com, which is one of the most popular shows on the site. She wrote the popular "Career Track" column for the *Washington Post* business section for three years.